A personal journey through shadow and light

Pete Barry

To Lorraine

Best Wishes

Pete Barry

Published by New Generation Publishing in 2017

Copyright © Pete Barry 2017

First Edition

The author asserts the moral right under the Copyright, Designs and Patents Act 1988 to be identified as the author of this work.

All Rights reserved. No part of this publication may be reproduced, stored in a retrieval system or transmitted, in any form or by any means without the prior consent of the author, nor be otherwise circulated in any form of binding or cover other than that in which it is published and without a similar condition being imposed on the subsequent purchaser.

www.newgeneration-publishing.com

Thanks to everyone and all the places I have investigated through my life so far. There are too many people to thank who have helped me along the way.

There is only one person that I dedicate this book to and that is Caroline Clare my mentor and friend.

Contents

INTRODUCTION 1
THE EARLY YEARS 3
GROWING UP 12
THE HALLS OF RESIDENCE 23
THE LATER YEARS AT THE HALLS 31
THE INN ON THE MOOR 36
WHAT HAPPENED NEXT 52
GREECE 56
A VERY BUSY TIME AHEAD 64
OUT WITH OLD AND IN WITH THE NEW 74
DAD'S PASSING 93
MOVING ON 101
THE ASHES SAGA 112
ONWARDS AND UPWARDS 114
LEARNING FROM SPIRIT 127
MUM AND DAD'S FINAL JOURNEY 139
LEARNING TO TRUST IN SPIRIT 145
GHOST HUNTING BACK ON THE AGENDA 153
AMAZING AND LIFE SAVING OCCURRENCES ... 181
MY ABILITIES ARE TESTED 189
THE RIGHT GROUPS 196

Introduction

This is an autobiography of my life up to the present day, which I hope you will enjoy.

It is more than amazing the life I have been living for many years now and not until I started to write this did I realise just how much. I thought my life was pretty mundane and ordinary with many disappointments along the way. The negativity around me has been overwhelming at times and you don't see the good in yourself until you recall what you have done with your life. If along the way my life story helps you in any way, it has done its job.

I'm just a run of the mill 56-year-old man with an extraordinary tale to tell.

You will see as I write this account of various aspects of my life that it has been less than ordinary.

Exciting and fascinating throughout and carrying a message we can all learn from, I feel.

I believe we are on a spiritual path from the day we are born until the day we pass over and beyond.

From being one of the world's biggest sceptics about anything spiritual to a practicing medium has been quite an emotional roller coaster ride.

I am putting pen to paper now to share this series of life changing events with you.

From ghost sightings to ghost hunting and mediumship development, I hope you will stay with me and we can enjoy the ride together.

Some of you may be able to relate to some of the situations I have found myself in over the years and may want to investigate them further on your own life path.

I will try and make this book as humorous as possible but it carries a very strong message that there is more out there than we understand at present.

We all have this little voice in our heads (our higher self), which tells us what is right and what is wrong. If it feels right, carry on and if it feels wrong, don't do it.

I wish I had trusted in it over the years in hindsight and I have met many fascinating and interesting people over the years that have helped me along the way.

I really needed help at times when things were going a little crazy and found people more than willing to assist me.

I hope my life continues on the path I find myself right now, as it is my world and we are all individuals so believe in what you believe and don't let others ridicule you or bring you down. It's your life, so live it your way.

The Early Years

Thinking back, growing up, my life was more than a little strange.

I was born in May 1959 in a Belfast hospital during the worst thunder and lightening storm in their history with temperatures soaring to the upper nineties. There were many complications with the birth procedure and by all accounts I should not have survived.

The air was electrically charged that night so did this have a bearing on how my future would turn out? Who knows?

We left Belfast when I was one year old (so I don't remember a thing) and moved to Dovercourt in Essex.

My earliest memory was when I was under three years old playing with a wooden push along train in a small house in Bognor Regis while on holiday but why that memory I wonder?

I was told while being watched by my mum that my eyes would follow things around the room and I would point even before I had learnt to speak.

I would be heard talking to things that no one else could see when I was only a little older and by the age of five, I had an imaginary friend called Peter and boy was he trouble!

The things he did you would not believe, but it was my backside and ears that usually bore the brunt of his misdemeanours so I just wonder now if he was an imaginary friend after all or a spirit. I will never know, but I have my suspicions to this day.

We moved to Leicester when I was five and then strange things started to happen soon after we moved in.

It was a big old house in the Evington area, which I never liked from the first time I crossed the threshold and this was the first time I had a strange feeling we were not alone in this place.

I told Mum and Dad that I did not like the place and

asked if we could move somewhere else, which went down really well but being told not to be stupid I ventured in through the front door and into the abyss.

It was huge and I was only little at about four feet tall at the time but

I had to admit what a place to grow up in, though hindsight is a wonderful thing. The garden was large with loads of grass for playing football on and a raised level with raspberry bushes neatly planted in rows where we would spend many hours picking fruit. To the left was a WWII air raid shelter still intact with a vegetable plot above it. I loved the garden and actually preferred it to the house with good reason, as you will find out.

As you walked in through the front porch there was another door into the hallway with a large imposing staircase in front of you. There was a landing half way up before bending left to the top of the stairs and the upstairs corridor with two bedrooms off on the left, one in front of you and one down the far end of the dark gloomy corridor, which belonged to my parents. Further along the corridor was a separate toilet and bathroom, which we will be coming back to.

Downstairs felt much nicer with a large lounge, a dining room and separate kitchen with a pantry, which lead along a covered alleyway to the garage and an outside toilet, which housed more spiders than you could shake a stick at.

Funny how I always seemed to end up in that hell hole when there was a nice cushy one upstairs even in winter and I remember once the milkman (yes we had them in those days) kept using the outside toilet without asking, so Mum, in her infinite wisdom, placed cling film (a precious new commodity) over the seat and funnily enough he never used it again but I digress. That's the tour over now so down to business.

Once I put my foot on that first step of the stairs when I was on my own I really felt I was on my own. At the far end of that long corridor was Mum and Dads bedroom and very imposing it was too. Not only because it was Mum and Dads and a no go area for us. We moved in properly and upstairs, though terrifying, was just about acceptable to me, my brother and sister but the bathroom I hated full stop. The least amount of time I spent in there, the better, but the toilet seemed ok. Once when I was on my own upstairs and I had managed to commandeer the posh loo I heard footsteps coming up the stairs and along the corridor that seemed to stop outside the toilet. I could hear heavy laboured breathing and then the footsteps headed off toward my parents bedroom so I was out of there like a shot. I can't remember whether I used the toilet paper but I was at the bottom of the stairs before I realized where I was and petrified I ran into the garden as I did not want to go back in to that house at any cost. That was really the start for me and things rapidly took a turn for the worse and unbeknowing to me, my brother and sister were experiencing similar occurrences but said nothing as they did not want to scare me. Too late!

The bathroom seemed to be the hub of the activity for all of us though again none of us said anything to each other. Whenever I had a bath my back had to be against the taps as there was a small window above the bathroom door and I felt I was being watched by someone. In later years my sister was to tell me she did exactly the same for similar reasons.

Once the landing and corridor lights went off at night, terror gripped me as I did not feel safe and I usually ended up in somebody else's bed (I was still very young) for some form of security. Something was very wrong with this house and we knew it (in later years we were to find out that a reclusive old man had died in Mum and Dad's bedroom) but my parents never experienced him, or so they said, but I'm not so sure. Did this old chap have an affinity with young children that doesn't bear thinking about now? What a horrible thought.

Mum came from a water milling background in Suffolk. Born in Thorrington Street and brought up in

Thorrington Street Mill along with her brothers. Ron died from a bike accident three days before his twenty first birthday and how traumatic must that have been for her and I mention this now, as a reference will occur later. In the upstairs corridor opposite the bathroom was a picture of Mum in her wedding dress looking out onto the river Stour at Boxsted Mill, where apparently a girl had drowned in the floods years before. A beautiful picture for sure, but it scared the life out of us kids. Could this be connected to the strange goings on in our house? None of us were quite sure.

The phone, a great big mustard coloured monstrosity at the bottom of the stairs had, on many occasions, rang when I was in the house and either silence or a similar heavy breathing to the one I had heard upstairs greeted me when I answered it. It made me too scared to answer the phone and when it did ring I would find myself too busy to answer it or as far away from it as possible and if you read this in a book you wouldn't believe it (oops, sorry you are).

Many times I flooded the upstairs bathroom floor as I was having a wash and had left the taps running as I had heard a voice or felt someone standing behind me which made me run downstairs and make conversation with Mum and Dad or who ever was available at the time just so I did not have to go back up those stairs again. Then would come the familiar drip, drip, drip, through the ceiling as water from the hand washing sink spilled on to the floor where I had left the taps running. This happened on more than one occasion. Dad would charge upstairs to see what damage I had caused this time as the lights started to flicker from the water damage and I would be in the doghouse once again but sooner that, than face the bathroom from hell. My brother would, in later years, carry out lone vigils at the top of the stairs (more fool him I say).

I really looked forward to the word "holiday" as it meant I could escape from the haunted house and down to

Suffolk for a few weeks.

I loved going there to the water mills to visit my aunts and uncles on my mother's side of the family. We stayed in the beautiful picturesque village of Polstead, which in itself can tell many a tale.

We camped and caravanned on friend's land in a cherry orchard and yes, we did eat quite a few. Auntie Dorry and Uncle Les were always the perfect hosts and a big part of my childhood.

At night we would listen for the nightingale. The stars were an awesome sight and Dad was the astronomer in the family and knew everything there was to know about these heavenly bodies and Mum was Mum and as kids we knew it.

I was the fisherman in the family and where that came from nobody seems to know. Polstead had a lovely pond for fishing at the bottom of a long steep winding hill and it was beautiful there and the sun always seemed to shine in those days. Off I would go with my fishing rod and basket over my shoulder at first light listening to the wood pigeons cooing in the trees and the ducks quacking in the distance thinking to myself life could not get any better than this. Just before the pond on the left hand side was a building I was drawn to, yet I had that feeling you get when all is not well, and this was becoming quite common with me now. It was a very old building built in the Tudor style and I knew there was something strange about it right from the word go. Opposite the pond was Polstead Church with its graveyard, which will crop up again during this book. It was hidden amongst the trees and the only give away was the bells, which you could hear peeling periodically. Polstead was a place you could wander at will without fear of being molested and you had more chance of falling in the lake and drowning than anything else, but this had not always been the case when I found out about the Red Barn Murder.

Maria Marten was a young girl who was befriended by a man from Polstead village who planned to elope with her and his name was William Corder. He arranged to meet her at the Red Barn where he murdered her instead and hid her body, which was later found. Corder was found guilty of the charge and as a result was hung, drawn and quartered for his actions. His skin was later used to bind a book, ironically based on the story of Maria's murder, which is still on show to this day in Bury St. Edmunds Museum. He had lived in the same house in Polstead village that struck fear into me every time I passed it, so was this the stirrings of some strange ability that I possess to communicate with spirit?

Thorrington Street Mill was the quintessential English architectural gem, sat at the side of the beautiful crystal clear river Box and it had been in the Munson family for over a century but sadly no longer and it now belongs to a private Trust. Below the mill was a crystal clear mill pool full of fat hungry rainbow trout that I fed with bread, much to the disgust of the local fly fishermen who were paying a premium to fish such a fine stretch of river. Occasionally you would see a flash of electric blue as a kingfisher skimmed the surface of the river in search of its quarry. The mill wheel was at the side of the old mill house but no longer turned as production had ceased many years before. Even as a child, that area made me very nervous and with a touch of sadness and although there was a chicken run further down, I would not venture there as I just didn't like the back of the mill. Whenever I peered into the millrace and the deep clear mill pool I felt like I wanted to fall in. How strange I should feel like this or was it overactive imagination as dad would say? Not in this case, as history revealed the previous owner before the Munson's the Scowen's suffered tragedy there. Mr. Scowen became very unhappy and depressed and eventually took his own life. He slit his own throat and was found by his daughter on the floor of the mill house bathroom who ran for help but on her return could not find her father. He had managed to crawl out of the house along the path at the back of the mill and thrown himself into the mill pool where his life had ended. No wonder I didn't like it round there and another example of my ability to sense spirits even at that age.

Thorrington Street Mill is currently spelt Thorington following a name change in recent years. This was one of Mum's biggest bugbears and out of respect to her and all the Munson's I am using the original spelling as it feels right. I think Mum may be whispering in my ear, so I better listen.

The house attached to the mill belonged to my Uncle Joe (Mum's remaining brother) and his wife my Auntie Pansy and whenever the mill was mentioned or a trip to it I would prick up my ears and get rather excited. During the day it was all about feeding and watching the trout or walking along the riverbank and across the cornfields ripened by the summer sun until a tea of salad and cakes became available in the evening. Sometimes hares could be seen boxing in the field from the front windows, while swallows were busy building mud nests under the eaves of the old mill. At dusk bats would suddenly appear from nowhere swooping and turning sharply to catch unsuspecting flies and other insects. It was such a marvellous scene and what a place to spend our holidays but eventually we were all snuggled up in the lounge and I listened intently to the family tales when suddenly a figure would appear somewhere in the room who really shouldn't have been there but what did I know at that age. I would butt into the conversation and ask whom the person was standing in the corner and Dad would respond by saying, "Shut up and don't be so stupid", but Mum would turn a funny shade of pale grey or even white when I gave out the descriptions of these people and you must remember this was Mum's side of the family and she knew them all. So as not to upset Dad, she would change the subject very quickly and it was suddenly time to go, always sooner than expected.

This was a common occurrence when we visited the mill and became quite a game for me. I thought it was fun as I was only a kid after all at the time, though it never seemed to be mentioned after the event until one day Pansy and Joe told how a few nights previous they had swerved to avoid a man who crossed in front of their car an old Triumph Herald. They stopped the car and got out, but nobody or damage to the car was found. They put it down to the fact it must have been a ghost. I had given full descriptions of people in the mill and all I got was "It's your over active imagination son" from my Dad.

"So unfair" as teenagers would say these days.

At this time they should have realised I was no ordinary child. While at school, I was a bit of a loner and enjoyed my own company.

I was never bullied, probably because they may have thought I had the capabilities of putting a hex on them, and I quite often would have conversations with people who were not visible to the human eye. Seeing this from the classroom door they may have thought 'well he's better off left alone'.

The very next day, by chance, my Dad read an article about the local vicar having been driven out of the Vicarage by a rampant poltergeist. The house had been moved from the top of the hill on rollers to a new site further down the hill and this fascinated me, an amazing feat that would have been awesome to see.

"Dad. What's a poltergeist?" I asked, which took him rather by surprise, my usual off the cuff type of question. It sounded like the name of some domestic fowl and trust me there were plenty in the area.

When he had explained the best he could I became very interested even at that tender age about this incident, while other kids were out walking, riding bikes etc. as TV's were rare and computers not even heard of in the domestic situation.

He embellished the story by relaying the ghostly tale of the headless horseman and carriage that was supposedly seen at night on this same stretch of road that runs for a mile and a half towards the Red Barn. Suddenly Dad said,

"I will give you ten pounds if you walk that stretch of road alone and I will pick you up at the other end."

In those days that was a small fortune and although I had a fascination with ghosts there was no way was I walking that road alone in the dead of night, which he was quite disappointed about, I said,

"You do it then" and I received a clip round the ear so I already knew his answer. Though I didn't go through with it, this heightened my interest in the paranormal and on the way back to Polstead from Stoke by Nayland, Dad decided to detour by the site of the Red Barn, which no longer stood as it had been destroyed by gruesome souvenir hunters over the centuries. As we pulled up, I caught the glimpse of a young woman disappearing around the corner of a farm building and I noticed she was dressed in what I would now describe as period costume. I got out of the car and ran to where I had seen her but there was no one there. I felt a cold chill, rather like those I experienced back at home in the haunted house but should I tell Dad what I had seen? Not wishing for another clip round the ear, I stayed quiet. We shuffled around for a bit but then got back in the car and returned to the cherry orchard.

It was a lovely place to stay, but all good things have to come to an end and soon it was time to return to the haunted house as I called it. The journey home was long and slow, the way I liked it personally when you knew what was at the other end waiting for you.

As soon as we pulled up on the drive my mood would change, though I don't think the rest of the family ever noticed it.

Odd issues occurred on and off over the next few months but nothing really out of the norm, so life seemed to return too normal or as best it could anyway.

I'm not using days and dates in this book as I'm not sure of them. Anyway I just remember the way things happened and the next series of events have left a marked impression on me forever and could be one of the reasons I started ghost hunting as a result.

Growing Up

It was one Christmas and everyone was in high spirits (pardon the pun), presents were being unwrapped and this didn't take long in those days, not like today where kids have everything and money seems to be no object in some households, but we were grateful for anything we received. I can't remember what I got but it was probably some new fishing tackle while my brother had one parcel, which kept drawing my attention, and I was intrigued to find out what it was. As he ripped the paper off I remembered seeing the words OUIJA on the box and a shudder went down my spine, I didn't know what one was but I didn't like it for some reason. He seemed delighted with his present (each to their own) and soon he had the board on the table with the planchette on top as he told me that was what it was called. I don't know why, but the thing terrified me and when my brother said, "it's used to communicate with the dead" I didn't know what to make of it, but I kept away.

Anyway, Christmas dinner came and went which was always a major event in our house and things calmed down and as usual the Queen's Speech was patriotically observed as always and Mum and Dad were asleep with Christmas hats on after a large meal and a dose of sherry and other alcoholic beverages having taken their toll. My brother and sister were in the dining room doing something but I didn't know what, so I went to investigate and left parents in their current state of slumber in the large lounge. As I entered into the dining room I was told to

"Sit down and shut up if you're going to watch" (brother and sisterly love) so I did. Both had their fingers on a heart shaped object on top of a board with letters and numbers on and were asking all sorts of questions to it and I found this a strange state of affairs and I had no desire to join in, even if I was asked too and like that was going to happen! Nothing really happened during that session and soon it was packed back into its box where it should have stayed.

The rest of the day passed without incident as the television now took centre stage and alcohol once again along with mince pies, a bowl of nuts with nutcrackers were the order of the remains of the day.

Boxing Day was really the start of what was to come and remember the house was already haunted in our opinion and during the afternoon my brother and sister, Mum but I can't remember if Dad joined in (I think he had more sense bless him) got the dreaded board out again. They seemed to being enjoying themselves when suddenly things changed,

I had just slid silently into the room and sat down when this happened.

"Is there anybody there"?
"Yes"
"What is your name"?
"Ron"
"How old were you when you died"?
"Nearly 21 years"
"How did you die"?
"Bicycle accident"

Dates and names followed and all I can remember is Mum bursting into tears and leaving the room screaming,

"How could you be so cruel and nasty stop it now!" towards my brother and sister. When she had calmed a few hours later, my brother and sister spoke to her saying they had not fooled her and everything had come through the board but she still did not believe them. I was still fairly young and to see my Mum in such a state terrified me as Mum was the strong one and nothing fazed her but this sure had. I was in tears as well and now I feared this board had infiltrated our house and there was enough spooky goings on in the place without any extras thank you very much.

Next time the board came out I started crying and

screaming,
"Don't use it",
I kept this up for hours until Dad stepped in and said,
"We will burn it", well that was the shortest Christmas present in history I thought, but I wasn't bothered my fishing tackle was ghost free anyway.

I calmed right down knowing the 'dead board' was no longer an issue as I now called it but oh boy was I proved to be wrong.

Anyway this set of circumstances had taken my mind off what lurked upstairs in the haunted house for now and it seems funny that the WWII air raid shelter in the back garden, which you would think, would be haunted if anything was going to be just wasn't. I played in the garden for hours day and night and never saw anything strange but it was eventually demolished as it had started to decay and became too unsafe to play in any longer. Such a shame as we were so lucky to have such a bomb proof den.

I was not aware at the time but the 'dead board' was still full of life or possibly death, as it had been put away with me given the knowledge it had been burnt.

The next night the "dead board" was to leave the house as Mum and Dad were taking it to a friend's house up the road for a session and as you can now see the evil board was starting to take control in its own way but little did I know that I was to be the target.

My brother and sister had the pleasure of babysitting me, as I was still too young to be left alone and I had gone up to bed because in those days even at holiday time bedtime was eight o'clock no questions asked. My brother and sister had settled down to watch a film on the TV and I, as ever, was left alone upstairs with the spooks.

There was a different kind of feeling in my bedroom when it suddenly went very cold and strange shadows seemed to dance around the walls and there didn't seem to be much of a breeze to blow the curtains either and no windows were open. I pulled up the covers, as I felt more than a little uncomfortable, when suddenly I heard what I can only describe to this day as long fingernails being dragged down the window pane and then a voice I will never forget asking me all sorts of questions as the curtains blew violently after calling my name which was something I have never forgotten. I let out the largest blood curdling scream ever and told my brother to stop it, as I needed an explanation and quickly too, for my sanity. I heard the downstairs door open and my brother came charging up the stairs asking what the hell was going on but I could not speak. I was petrified literally, traumatized and any other description you care to give. I was a shivering wreck in fits of hysteria as my brother tried to calm me down. The voice was pure evil nothing like I had experienced in the haunted house before and there were no trees outside the upstairs front window so what had dragged its fingernails down the glass like nails on a chalkboard?

I slept with the lights on that night and the upstairs resembled a lighthouse with good reason. Mum and Dad came back around two o'clock in the morning and demanded an explanation from my brother, but this was withheld until the following day.

The following morning seemed far away but I fell asleep somehow and soon it was daylight and once again comparative safety for now.

I came down for breakfast and the air was tense and it looked like big brother was well and truly in the doghouse instead of me for a change but I still had to explain what had happened during the night and again Mr over active imagination got the blame until Mum and Dad asked me what the questions were that I had been asked while they were out.

They sat there open mouthed when they started to realize that the questions were the same as they had asked through the 'dead board' at friends at the top of the road possibly a dozen houses away.

Dad checked the bedroom and nothing was found of any consequence, my brother was pardoned and the 'dead board' was unceremoniously burnt much to my delight in the back garden.

Most people who have been on my ghost investigations know I don't use Ouija Boards and never will again and now you know the reasons why and that was exactly as it happened so it's up to you if you heed my advice or not but if you do please open and close them properly.

What started out as a parlour game turned into a life changing experience and a Christmas I will never forget. Some of you may listen to my words and some may say rubbish but you have to decide.

Everything that is written in this book has actually happened to me over the years and that's what makes this journey so fascinating.

The very same evening after the inquest I was laying on my bed reading the Sports Mercury as that's how you got your reports of football matches in those days, when something dropped from the ceiling onto the middle of the open paper and as I peered down I was off the bed in a flash as a rather oversized house spider was looking at me and as I don't like spiders that rounded off those sequence of events rather nicely I felt.

Once the board was burnt I felt much more at ease and things seemed to settle down for a period of time but the next event though I don't really remember much about it and nearly cost me my life by all accounts and could be another reason spirits are close to me now.

I love my fishing and when I couldn't get to the canal I would even go fishing for sticklebacks in the local brook armed with a net and a large jam jar. Mum would pack me up some sandwiches and off I would go on my quest to capture a jar of these orange, red and blue spiny little fish. The brook had been in flood and was a dirty chocolate brown colour and still nearly bank high but that didn't deter me as I was there to catch fish. I had caught nothing in my net and I was now getting hungry so I sat down in the long grass to eat my sandwiches and there was never a thought given to washing my hands first. When a river is in flood it washes out the rat holes in the bank, which are full of their urine, and transmits it to the water and that way it can be passed on to humans as I was shortly to find out. After a less than fruitful day I returned home later that afternoon feeling fine and it wasn't until a few days later that I started to develop the symptoms of a cold but it wasn't particularly bad at that time and as I was due to go to Mablethorpe with the cubs (the younger version of the scouts) and nothing was going to stop me. The day came and I was off on the coach for a week away with the rest of the boys for a jolly old time or so I thought but that was to change very quickly as within a couple of days the cold was getting worse and my breathing was starting to feel a little compromised. I had little or no energy to speak of and the cub pack leader was getting very concerned as I didn't want to go anywhere or do anything and remember I was on holiday a time when you should be enjoying yourself. Eventually they rang my parent's and said,

"I think Pete should go home as he doesn't want to join in any of the planned activities and is spoiling it for the rest," which was not how it was at all. I remember being bundled into a car with all my stuff and being driven back home though I don't remember the trip. When my parents saw me they sent me straight to bed and the emergency doctor was called immediately as I looked like death warmed up and that's how I felt. I remember nothing after that for quite a while until Dad came in from work carrying a large plastic crocodile with wheels, which he gave to me with probably the biggest smile on his face I had ever seen. Apparently when the doctor arrived my condition was desperate and time was running out unless they could find out what it was and he told my parent's in the downstairs kitchen,

"If we don't find a cure for this you will not have your son in six hours", very blunt but true apparently. It was then Mum said,

"Just before it started he had been fishing in the local brook and could he have caught something there,"

Doctor, "I've heard of Weils Disease that is spread though water by rats but I have never come across it before,"

Mum, "Please doctor try anything, I'm losing my son and no parent should see any of their children buried",

At that point the doctor pumped everything he could think of into me and by some miracle it worked and though recovery was slow at least I had survived the ordeal. There were after effects for a couple of months and yes I did fish in the brook again but I never took sandwiches with me and always washed my hands after. I don't think it was anything to do with the house by the way, but it was another time of shadow in my life.

Sometime later when I had fully recovered I had gone fishing with a friend up the local Grand Union Canal and my brother was home alone. He was on the upstairs posh loo, which I never seemed to get to use when he heard a door go downstairs and heavy footsteps climbing up the stairs and along the corridor towards parents bedroom. He shouted out,

"What you doing back" but there was no reply. Déjà vu as I had had a similar experience as I mentioned before. I was happily pulling out tench (lovely green fish with bright red eyes) from the canal miles away with not a care in the world and being inquisitive by nature he set out his stall to capture this ghost somehow and whenever we went away and he stayed behind with the house to himself I don't know what he did to try and capture this spirit but it would have been fun to watch.

One day the local vicar rang (yes the phone did ring occasionally for legitimate reasons) and asked if he could pay Mum a visit just for a chat. I don't think she was over keen thinking back as the church curate lived over the fence and was a very good friend but Mum being Mum she duly obliged and invited him round.

I was read the riot act about being on my best behaviour on pain of death (children should be seen and not heard but in my case not seen either when we had visitors of any importance) as Mum was always doing things for the church as usual but it wasn't me she needed to worry about.

The house was spotless as usual except for my bedroom and the smell of fresh baked cakes wafted through the house and permeated the air. The doorbell rang and in came our special guest who was taken into the lounge. Things went rather well and sitting half way up the stairs listening, as there was no way I was sitting at the top for fear of personal safety. I could hear laughter and things seemed to be going ok and cakes were being devoured with cup after cup of tea but something did not like the vicar enjoying himself in our house and devised a diversion.

In the kitchen was a gas stove that we used to light with matches (none of those clickey gadgets in our day), which were kept at the side of the stove. These were safety matches for that reason in a very large box and about a foot above was a hanging tea towel. Suddenly I could smell burning as the safety matches had caught fire (how you may ask) and then the tea towel went up and a fire had started. I ran downstairs to try and put it out but the flames just got higher and there was now a serious risk of having to call the fire brigade but Dad heard my cries and came dashing into the kitchen and somehow beat the flames back to gain control in a very heroic manner, which resulted in the vicar hurriedly leaving and another inquest began which I got the blame as you would expect but I know it wasn't me.

Someone or something had taken a dislike to a vicar being on the premises and needed rid of him and if I had not been there perhaps the haunted house would have burned down and what thanks did I get, grounded for what felt like an eternity. The kitchen had to be redecorated due to smoke damage and that was all in the end so we were lucky as it could have been far worse. Fires became a bit of a theme with small ones breaking out occasionally but were always found to have a logical explanation behind them. I just wonder whether the spirit still resides there but do I really care?

That house was a real learning curve for me and one November a strange one started which I will now relate. A bit of stupidity on my part for playing the game in the first place though.

We did not have fireworks, as we grew older we felt they were a waste of money and bought more constructive items with the money Mum and Dad gave us but I always liked Bengal Matches (matches again) which lit up all bright colours when struck. It was night time and they showed up better in the dark, especially when thrown from an upstairs window. My friend from across the road (yes I had one) decided to have a competition to see who could chuck one the furthest. Curtains were drawn, the night was cold and still so we let battle commence and as we had two full boxes of matches alternate throws were to be the order of the day. Competition went well until the last match which was mine and this was my chance to claim the bragging rights for the year. Every match so far had left a blazing trail and travelled some distance so I gave it some force like all the others but it seemed to have a mind of its own and it was like some invisible force had picked it up and was determined to do some damage with it. It was still cold with no breeze and a frost on the ground so why was it acting so strangely as it seemed to fly for much longer than any of the others. When it finally landed it was against the side of the house still smouldering away and set light to the television cables and very quickly became angry and some rubbish I hadn't noticed there before. We both ran downstairs towards this raging inferno and somehow managed to find a bucket of stagnant water, which quelled the flames more by luck than anything else. Another close shave, especially as the matches had been thrown from the window the fingernails had scraped down a few years ago and scared the life out of me but of course the next day, when Dad found the aftermath, we both denied all knowledge and Dad put it down to a cable fault and had them replaced, phew that was a let off.

One last strange incident occurred in that house that I can remember clearly and I probably still have the bumps and bruises to prove it.

I woke up one night in the early hours and the bedroom was pitch black which was unusual because there was always a streetlight or some other light source finding its way in the room but on this occasion there wasn't. I'd woken as I needed the toilet and I needed to go right then but I never put the bedroom or landing light on so as not to wake anybody. I got out of bed and groped my way towards the door as I had done many times before without a problem. On the other side of the door was the big thick bannister rail that ran for eight feet or so to the opening at the top of the stairs with steps down to the middle landing and then swept right again to the hallway below. Still holding onto the door I reached for the bannister but it just wasn't there and I found myself tumbling and falling down the stairs, which woke the whole household anyway so I might as well have put the lights on in the first place. I tumbled into the large carboy, (a large glass bottle for keeping plants in) and into the wall below the stained glass window in a pure state of shock. I didn't break any bones or dislocate anything but I still to this day can't understand how it happened. There was no way I could reach the gap at the top of the stairs while holding onto the bedroom door so what had happened, I guess I will never know.

As we grew older we all moved away from home taking with us the memories of the haunted house so I thought that would be the end of ghostly adventures for me but I'm afraid it was only the beginning but it stood me in good stead for what was to follow.

By the way Mum and Dad eventually sold the haunted house to some poor unsuspecting fools and it was wasn't long before the new owners felt the wrath of that house. It wasn't that they kept in touch with the new owners but they read in the local paper that the house had gone up in flames two weeks after they had vacated it.

Nobody was injured thank goodness, as the house was empty at the time but it makes you think. The roof was completely destroyed and had to be replaced and it makes you think after all the brushes we had with fires while living there.

The Halls of Residence

From when I left the haunted house to the time I started work as a chef in the halls not a great amount of strange or spiritual activity happened. Maybe I had strayed off my life path or had not been listening to my higher self but all that was about to change.

I had taken up a job in student halls, which came with living accommodation, which I might add I was very grateful for at the time. The building that was to be my home for a few years was imposing to say the least and built probably at the turn of the nineteenth century. It was in an area surrounded by very large houses that would at one time have had butlers and servants for sure. It was in a very affluent area of Leicester with a rich history and they had now been bought up to be used for student accommodation which seemed a bit of a shame as these sorts of places in my opinion really needed some loving care and attention but I had a job and somewhere new and exciting to live so all was good.

I moved into a small temporary student room in the main part of the building as the flat above the offices was not yet ready for me to live in. You entered the building through a big heavy oak front door and there were many doors off to the left and right, a massive staircase that bent round and would not have looked out of place in a stately home loomed in front of me. There were small student rooms dotted around the upper level with a few offices and reception areas, while my temporary accommodation was a pokey little room tucked away in a corner of the upstairs landing. It was still the backend of summer and the students were still on vacation so all was quiet and I had the place to myself, or so I thought, as I moved my worldly possessions into my new accommodation and settled into my new life.

It was still a bright and sunny day so I went for a walk around the massive site across lush green lawns and along gravel paths. I thought how lucky I was to be living in a place like this but as I have said before hindsight is a wonderful thing.

Squirrels were jumping from tree to tree and running up the gnarled old oaks and conifer trees. Wood pigeons were cooing in the trees which reminded me of my holidays in Polstead now long gone and walking past Corder's Cottage to the big fishing pond. The air was full of bees, which seemed to be on every flower busily collecting pollen while windfall apples and pears had started to drop and angry wasps would warn you off from their stache of rich fermented fruit. I loved being at one with nature and, as I have said before, I enjoyed my own company. This was heaven to me as I lost myself to the sights, sounds and smells of the autumn so what could go wrong I thought, as it seemed too good to be true to be living here.

Being autumn, the nights were drawing in and soon bats were wheeling overhead. The sounds of owls hooting in the trees could be heard and I had lost track of time being in this wonderland which was soon to be unleashed once again on marauding students.

I opened the creaking heavy old oak door and made my way back up the majestic staircase. (This is all well and good you may say but where are the ghosts), be patient as it started all too quickly for my liking. I went into my room put the kettle on and then started to realise I was alone and very alone in this nineteenth century house.

I was going to have a shower before heading for bed but thought better of it as downstairs now took on a rather sinister appearance and the first thoughts in many years of the haunted house I used to live in flooded back into my head. Don't be silly, I thought that was a one off, but how wrong could I be.

I switched the lights off outside the room and dived into probably the most uncomfortable bed I have ever slept in as the watery moon was piercing the curtains and I suddenly felt I was not alone. This was the first time I had really been on my own in years and thoughts of the

Suffolk Lane that Dad had offered me ten pounds to walk down pounded in my head. It must have been about two o'clock in the morning when I was awoken by someone or something knocking on the big old oak door downstairs. Rap, rap, and rap so I pulled the covers up tight around me and tried to ignore this disconcerting sound. I remembered Dad's words "overactive imagination" until it happened again. Rap, rap, rap so who would be banging the door at this time of night? I had to find out.

I got out of bed and headed down the stairs when I heard another rap on the door, which quite startled me as I unbolted the big heavy oak door and opened it to find nobody was there. I felt like I was in a horror movie and the door had only just been knocked and there was an active security light outside which had not been activated by anything. I waved my hand in front of it and the light came on and did not go off for approximately two minutes. What was it that had banged the door so vigorously that first night? Nothing else happened though I certainly did not sleep like a baby I can assure you.

I woke up bleary eyed about nine o'clock as I didn't start my employment until the following Monday which was the reason the self contained flat was not ready and right now I couldn't say I was looking forward to the next night.

I kept myself busy during the day and cooked myself something in the student kitchen downstairs and at one point I felt someone standing behind me, but of course, no one was there.

This was the Sunday and the next day I would be baptized into the ways of cooking for large numbers of students, who, by the way, would not start arriving back until the following Sunday. I must say it felt good to think that the next day I would be around other human beings but I had to survive the night first and all too soon it was getting dark and once again the building started to take on a sinister appearance. There was a strong wind blowing, which made things rattle and bang and even the strong old oak front door joined in and I thought well I could put any strange noises down to that for tonight.

How wrong was I when the landing light suddenly came on by itself and it wasn't on a timer but was the usual switch as in most households and light was flooding under my door. Shortly after I heard someone coming up the stairs with slow heavy footsteps and making a muffled humming sound. This brought memories flooding back of the haunted house I used to live in and I was frozen to the spot as the footsteps passed my door and then stopped. How could whoever or whatever it was go any further as I was in the end room so I flung the door open and no one was there and once again it was the only incident of the night that I could recall as I soon fell asleep somehow.

Monday morning arrived and I got a knock on my door from a real human being (thank the Lord) and it was the bursar who had been part of the interview panel come to take me to the kitchens for my first day. He pressed a key into my hand and said,

"That's to the flat I'm sure you don't want to stay here any more" winked and said nothing else. He had been there many years and knew all the tales there were to know and I don't know if I felt more joy starting my new job or being able to escape this hellhole. Yes, another one. It was only an introduction day in the kitchen and by four o'clock I was free for the day and one of the kitchen staff showed me to the flat, my very own self contained flat, wow!

I have never moved from one place to another in such a short space of time especially with the thought I had escaped the spooks, but how wrong I was once again.

The flat was all I wanted with a large lounge but not like the one in the haunted house, a kitchen, bath and shower room, a large bedroom with a spiral staircase up to it and corridor ran down to a small room at the bottom, which we will come to later.

Anyway I moved in and settled straight away and it couldn't have been more different from the ghost infested area I had just escaped from. Or was it? The central heating was good and quiet and being furnished it was rather posh by my standards so I felt at home here and the job in the kitchen was enjoyable I was finding.

Some of the girls in the kitchens would use the shower in my flat if they were going out in an evening, which I didn't mind really. Gradually a pattern started to emerge though, that when they hanged their clothes up items would go missing like tights, hairbrushes and socks. Trust me I was not above suspicion in this little mystery but what would I do with tights, hairbrushes and socks etc, (don't even go there!).

We worked shifts and one day one of the girls finished at two o'clock and I was on the late shift as usual and she went to use the shower.

When she had finished she came to put her clothes on but no dress or knickers could be found (I liked this ghost and it could hang around for as long as it wanted).

Next thing the girl came across the open courtyard to the kitchen wrapped in a towel to hide her modesty and started shouting that I was some kind of pervert and could she have her clothes back. She soon shut up when she realised I had been in a meeting with management for the last half hour and we nearly wet ourselves with laughter but what was causing these strange phenomena? Anyway she had to go home in the chefs uniform, which I found more than amusing as you do. Needless to say, the girls did not partake of using my shower again after that probably as it was getting too expensive for them.

No other issues occurred of any note for quite a while and for once I felt comfortable and the flat seemed quite friendly and on one occasion while talking to the bursar (as they were called in those days now better known as maintenance), I asked him what was in the room at the end of the corridor and he replied,

"We don't know as the key to that door was lost many years ago and I've been trying to get a key for it as it would be interesting to find out what lurks behind the door"

We left it like that for now but one day I was walking across the courtyard to work when the bursar said,

"Hey Pete, I've got a replacement key for the one that was missing to the spare room at the end of the corridor". We agreed to meet up later and further investigate the mystery room and so later that day with much excitement and trepidation we turned the key in the lock and it opened. It smelt very musty having been shut up for so long but what we caught site of took our breath away as on the bed were cans of hairspray, deodorant, hairbrushes, tights, knickers, socks and, of course, the girls party dress. Pete the pervert needed some apologies damn quickly and one very red-faced girl sidled off rather hurriedly with her dress and knickers and anything else she could carry and all objects were returned to their rightful owners including my collection of combs which I used in those days.

Looking back on it that was really funny and the look on the girls face was priceless and once that door had been opened nothing went missing again but things started to change rather rapidly shortly after in other areas.

I started having dreams at night or should I say nightmares about all sorts of things and I thought I could hear voices on many different occasions but I had the only key to the flat as when it was renovated it had had new locks in place. So who, or what, was moving stuff around in it? I would come in from work and find teacups on top of the television and clothes strewn on the floor, which started me thinking what the hell was going on. I started to be woken by bangs and tappings during the night which had not occurred before which I could never get to the bottom of but I had my suspicions about the room at the end of the corridor being opened.

When I took photographs in the flat with the new Kodak camera I had been bought (no digital in those days), strange mists and light anomalies were caught which I had no explanation for and it was as if something was trying to get my attention.

There was a bureau in the lounge with a top drawer at

one side that I could hardly use as when I tried to open it I would come up against a pillar but it opened far enough to keep my wallet and valuables in. One day I returned to the flat to find the draw upside down on the brown chair I sat on at the bureau. I panicked as I thought I had been burgled but to my relief when I turned the drawer over my wallet and valuables were still there along with my other valuables. I checked my wallet and found nothing was missing but how strange that there was no way you could put the drawer back in without heaving the bureau out completely and sliding the drawer back in then putting the bureau back. It made no sense as something with that power and ability could be dangerous and I was getting more than a trifle scared at this point and with good reason. My father came to visit one day and when we were standing at the lounge door a loud rasping sound was heard and a large stone with an elephant painted on it came off the TV onto the floor and picked up speed as it tumbled along before crashing into the lounge door at the side of us. Dad turned to me in a state of disbelief and said, "Its time you left this place. Very wise words indeed. I had told him of the goings on over recent times and until now he had taken it with a pinch of salt but not any more as he was genuinely scared for himself and me.

I met a girl called Lesley (later to be my wife and still is) who has experienced so many things with me and will verify most of what has happened with me in recent years and we decided to get a flat together somewhere else as she also did not like staying in this one either. How very wise.

It was the night before I was to move out when I saw something that really made me believe in ghosts not that I didn't already.

It was the early hours of the morning and very dark and I had been in a deep sleep when I awoke feeling very cold and I noticed a bright light in the corner getting brighter. A circle of light like a wonky wheel floated across the bedroom followed by the bright outline of a tall lady in a long flowing dress followed by yet another wonky wheel of pure bright light and they all dissipated through the wall and were gone. I was not scared, just fascinated and I was hoping they would come back but I'm afraid they never did. Why it happened, I will never know, but it gave me the thirst to carry out ghost hunts and help find the answers I, and many people crave.

We moved into the new flat and started a new chapter in our lives.

Whilst I was at the halls I got into badger watching out in the countryside with Lesley and as I usually found myself on late shifts it was an ideal time to venture out.

One night while out in the depths of the countryside watching a sett I saw a monk like figure striding across the ploughed field but Lesley could not see him as has happened on many occasions over the years but he was clear as day to me. I spoke to someone the next day about it who said up above where we where watching the badgers used to be an old abbey and fishponds which the local monks used.

I was beginning to realise I could see the dead and it wasn't my imagination and I wasn't only seeing I was sensing as well as I found out at another badger sett we were watching one night.

We had set up our little hide above a spinney that had a large badger sett in it and over to the left was an old Saxon church, which was a bit creepy I must admit in the dead of night. I turned my back to the church but I had a worse feeling coming from behind me now as if the dead were watching me. I found out later my back was to an Iron Age fort and burial ground and if I had known what was around the area I may have been a little less keen to badger watch there.

The later years at the halls

Once I had moved out of the halls I still carried on working there for quite a few years and strange occurrences were never far away in that place.

I remember two of us slicing meat on the electric slicers and having a jolly old time one day listening to the radio when both of us noticed at the same time the old metal round headed silver switch very slowly pushing upwards and finally the radio cutting out. We both looked at each other and uttered at the same time "Oh my God".

There was no logical explanation for this that we could come up with other than that particular spirit did not like our taste in music.

During the afternoon on a Saturday and Sunday I would often be on my own until the kitchen assistants arrived a few hours later and next to the kitchen was the large student dining room with a beautifully polished wooden floor. It had wooden double doors with glass windows at the far end. I always locked the doors as being on my own and working with knives, the public should be very scared of me (I know what you thought I was going to say) so nobody had access except the wardens and sub wardens who lived down the other end in the flats above.

Often I would hear loud and heavy footsteps walking up the hall every time I was alone and so many times I'd dropped everything and raced into the hall only to find it empty and then went upstairs to check on the wardens and not a soul was there in the physical anyway. Occasionally the toilet would flush while nobody was in there and it was only on a chain with no automatic flushing system, so it seemed as though when I was alone they wanted to play.

Perhaps the others were boring and not worth the effort and I wouldn't blame spirit for that as I worked with them but I must admit when you were on lock up at night the kitchen seemed to take on a different atmosphere.

During conference time we were moved around like

cattle to where the work was and across the road was now mainly for teas and coffees. I worked with a lovely lady called Mavis whom has since sadly passed to spirit and who my wife Lesley looked after being a nurse in hospital so she became more of a friend. She was the first person who really helped me to believe in what I was hearing and seeing, especially as one day I was washing up after a conference (chefs had to do that as well back then) when out of the corner of my eye came the impression of a man in an old style blue boiler suit but instead of a fleeting glance his body became more solid as if I were looking at you right now. He was not that old and gave me the impression of being an unhappy soul carrying emotional baggage and I felt like he wanted to speak but I didn't really understand at this time. I had played this game as I thought it was back then at Thorrington Mill in Suffolk as a very young boy. This was to turn out to be the first real validation I ever received while communicating with spirit and it came from the lovely Mavis.

With the description I gave Mavis later that day of this person she knew who it was straight away and tears welled up in her eyes. I felt bad as I hadn't meant to make a lady cry but as I was to learn they were not tears of sadness but relief and joy.

So at this stage I was very mixed up in my own mind with what was going on with me but I understood I was experiencing more ghostly activity than most people would encounter in a lifetime and apparently I could communicate with the dead without the aid of a much feared 'dead board'

I went about my daily routine but started seeing people in unusual places and would look again and they were gone.

Was it as in Dads words "overactive imagination" or something else?

One final incident that sticks in my mind before I finished working at the halls after nearly twenty years service took me completely by surprise.

Management had asked me to set up a tea and coffee station in a large old majestic building set back in the beautiful grounds which I always found eerie. I took what I needed with me and as I put the big old brass key in the lock I felt ok as it was a lovely sunny summers day and the students were on their summer vacations so there was no one about. I began laying out rows and rows of cups and saucers when I heard heavy footsteps on the wooden floor in the main corridor which I thought was strange at the time but I had deadlines to meet and I didn't have time to go and look what had caused them until the whistling started and the hackles started to rise on the back of my neck. Nobody should be in here I thought as I have the keys and I unlocked the building and this made me very nervous, but as I said previously I had deadlines to meet and eleven o'clock was that deadline and now it was approaching ten o'clock so I ignored the bangs and scrapings going on around me.

Everything was ready by twenty to eleven and no one was waiting for tea and coffee and they couldn't get in anyway as I had locked the door behind me and so I went for a bit of wander. Once again I heard the whistling and then that was followed by the toilet door closing. I thought, how has somebody got in and we weren't even open yet, so I waited a while as I could hear what I can only described as a man coughing and muttering to himself. I thought to myself I will grab him when he comes out and tell him that he should not be in here but I waited and waited and eventually I heard the toilet roll holder being unravelled and finally the chain being flushed and I thought I'm ready to collar this bloke, but nobody emerged from the toilet cubicle. In the end I was growing impatient so I went to knock on the door and as I did it just swung open and you guessed it no one was in there. I was rocked to my core as this really wasn't possible as I made my way quickly back to the service area and unlocked the door more to get a breath of fresh air than anything else. I tried to put the incident out of my mind while teas and coffees were being served and somehow I managed it in the end but I can't say I still didn't feel a little nervous.

Now it was time to clear away as service was finished and get out of the place once and for all, but one last surprise was to occur before I managed it. I was just drinking a steaming hot, well earned, cup of coffee when from the kitchen came a really loud rushing sound like taps being turned on fully, so I hurriedly put my coffee down and rushed to the kitchen. There was nothing to be seen and the noise had ceased as quickly as it had started. I checked the big deep stainless steel sinks and they were bone dry with no water residue and the taps were not even dripping and were tightly switched off. I didn't need to use the sinks anyway as the dishwashing machine, which was much larger than a domestic one, would cope with that amount of cups and saucers.

Nothing else happened and everything was left neat and tidy as I had found it and all I wanted to do now was to leave that place far behind. I started to walk out of the kitchen when I heard the rushing sound again and I turned around to see both taps blasting water into the deep stainless steel sinks. I was terrified right now but I had to turn the taps off so I went back over to the taps that were still blasting out water and I couldn't turn them off as they were locked that tightly on. I rang the maintenance department and one of the porters came quickly to site as this was a real issue that couldn't be left and a little bit of company wouldn't hurt right now. He went over to the sink and without any effort screwed the taps back into the off position and the water stopped. I felt such a fool but the porter just turned to me and said,

"He's tried that one before" and smiled.

I didn't want an explanation as I just wanted to get out of the place once and for all.

It was only a few days before I left for good but I dreaded that I would be asked to go in there again on my own so I tried to keep a low profile and look busy which I was pretty good at anyway.

As luck would have it I never needed to go back in and I still wonder to this day how many others have experienced things while working or living in that place as it is most definitely haunted in my opinion anyway.

The Inn on the moor

The summer holidays soon came around. I loved my holidays and this year the destination was to be Cornwall and we were camping again in the great outdoors with Mother Nature.

One place Lesley and I had always wanted to visit was Corfe Castle and so we made our way there traversing through some beautiful countryside along the way.

What a beautiful place. The views were stunning across Corfe itself and the valley down below when viewed from above up at the castle itself were breathtaking. Little puffs of white steam spouted from the funnel of the steam train slowly meandering and winding its way through the valley and you could hear the plaintive sound of its whistle echoing all around. Down below in Corfe Old town itself, where people milled around below like something out of a Lowry painting or a model railway scene was an awesome sight and better was to follow in the castle itself.

As we both entered the old town of Corfe, both of us had a feeling of déjà vu and seemed to know where we where in the place without the aid of any maps or previous visits. The castle seemed very easy for us to navigate which was strange when suddenly I was grabbed by two spirit soldiers who sat me down with a foaming flagon of ale (I wish) and said,

"We've been waiting along time for your return and we can drink again together",

Whether I was over tired I don't know but the place did feel uncannily real to me and all through the day, though the castle was busy, we both kept finding ourselves alone as if people were being diverted away from us for some unknown reason. All I knew was we had been there before, possibly in a previous existence but who knows in the great scheme of things. Towards the end of the visit we decided to go to the gift shop and after a good look round found nothing that we wanted to buy but decided to go to the attached café for a drink and some cake and as we went to sit down at the only free table I asked Lesley if I could sit where she was sitting for some reason, but I really didn't know why at that time.

While I was sitting in what should have been Lesley's seat I found I could see back into the gift shop at the only angle where I could see a long plastic packet hanging down that I had missed while walking around the shop. I was being drawn towards this little item so I had to satisfy my curiosity and take a look so I got up from the table and immediately spilled Lesley's coffee (much to her delight) in my haste. It was the only one left and I had to get it whatever it was as I was sure it was meant for me and as I reached the item and unhooked it from its peg I realised what I was holding was a set of divining rods. Why these of all things?

These items had always fascinated me and now I had my own pair and where these diving rods have taken me is a journey in itself and are still sometimes called upon in times of need.

I was always told that they were for finding water or ley lines but never in my wildest dreams did I realize they would aid in spiritual communication from the other side. I would have to teach them (sounds daft now) how they were to work for me first which was easier than I thought as spirit took control.

In my early days of communicating with spirit I learnt to rely on them and the accuracy they gave me was amazing and when I am running a ghost hunt they are a great visual tool. I will never regret the day spirit guided me towards them and, by the way, if you are ever out with me for a day and I ask you to swap seats because I'm not comfortable just think twice before accepting my offer.

Who would have thought a trip to a castle could have been so eventful and maybe even life changing but that's just what it turned out to be.

The next day armed with my divining rods I was pacing around all corners of the caravan and camping site (people must have thought I was a bit strange and not for the first time) trying to find water and anything else that might make the rods cross, with very little success.

I rack my brains now as I try and remember the first time spirit started to communicate with me using these items but I'm sure it was fairly soon after I purchased them but the finer details escape me I'm afraid now, but so much has gone on and I'm much older.

They will crop up at various locations and investigations throughout this book.

The holiday was turning out to be a great success and one day around Bodmin Moor we saw the sign for a famous Coaching Inn, so we took the turn and the oppressive looking building began to draw me in. We got a drink from the bar and mine was a lovely ice cold pint of cider with the condensation dripping down the side and onto the floor in the heat. We were sat at a small wooden table outside in the blistering heat, both of us in t-shirts and shorts as in anything else you would have been boiled alive. Suddenly I got the impression of two children one boy and one girl around me, and their energies were strong right now.

Whilst we were sitting there, I could see Lesley staring at the tops of my legs (this is not the time or place to be thinking like that my dear) but she was pointing and saying the hairs on the top of my legs were being brushed backwards and forwards by unseen hands. She had never seen anything like it before and was mesmerized (easily pleased that one) by the situation. To me it felt like a million money spiders running all over my legs and even when I got up it wouldn't stop. We walked towards the museum which was full of stuffed animals (now that's a bit creepy if I say so myself) but this sensation would not stop and it was driving me crazy. It must have looked like I had fleas or something as the man at the kiosk took our money and gave us our tickets and then said,

"You're ok they won't follow you upstairs" as if he knew who they were and that this was a regular occurrence. We went inside and it was morbid and creepy and I kept itching and scratching until as the man said you went upstairs and it worked, there were even more horrible exhibits upstairs but no cobwebbing effects. I could have stayed up there for a while and yet I did not like the place but I did not want that attack of the money spider's syndrome back at any cost. We came down the stairs and sure enough my faithful friends joined us once again so I went to have a chat with the guy who sold us the tickets but he was nowhere to be seen and I went in search of somebody else who might be able to shed some light on this and eventually I came across a manager and I asked him if the place was haunted and all he said with a smile on his face was,

"What do you think",

We came out into the courtyard and were met with bright sunshine still with my attachments but I was getting used to them by now and

as we walked to a quiet corner, all four of us (keep with me), I could hear children singing and playing and then suddenly they had gone along with my attachments.

I was missing them now they had gone and I actually felt slightly sad so whether that was impressed on me I don't know but it was another invaluable piece of the puzzle.

I just knew I had to come back to this amazing place sooner or later and sooner it was than I thought as for a surprise Lesley paid for us to stay there for my birthday.

That weekend changed my life and beliefs forever, as I shall explain and I probably wouldn't have been so keen to have gone if I'd known then what was about to happen or would I with my thirst for all things paranormal.

Well the day came and we were both up early and a couple of days off work helped anyway. The weekender bags were packed and my ghost hunting equipment that consisted of a digital camera and a night vision video camera were checked and ready (not like the arsenal of equipment I carry now) I'm afraid.

It was a lovely bright and sunny morning as we pulled out of the driveway for the long journey to Cornwall.

On the way down, we crossed Salisbury plain and made a small detour to visit Stonehenge as I had seen it on television and in pictures in books but I expected to see an immense array of huge stones pointing to the heavens in a large circle but I must say I was more than a little disappointed at the size of it. It was much smaller than I had imagined and it came as quite a shock and they say size isn't everything and on this occasion it really wasn't. Besides that, you weren't allowed to go anywhere near it, so feeling the earth energies or the spirits of the ancestors was out of the equation at this time.

Back on the road it had started to rain quite heavily now as we neared our destination. Everything was dripping wet as the sun popped back out to show the Inns slate grey facade glistening and shimmering in the late spring sunshine. As we pulled up to the old Coaching Inn, I felt we had company in the car with us and I wasn't wrong, as the two children I had encountered on our previous visit (attack of the money spiders) were with me once again. I thought this is going to be an interesting weekend, as we hadn't even got out of the car yet.

It was a large imposing building made of slate with large courtyard and a sign that was creaking in the wind, which sent a shiver down my spine, so we grabbed our bags, signed in and made our way up the narrow staircase past stuffed animals and other curiosities then along a narrow corridor with an uneven floor, which made you feel quite uneasy. At the end of the corridor there were rooms left and right and both reportedly haunted. Ours was to be the left hand one and would not let us down when it came to strange happenings.

As I pulled up the gun metal latch which rattled as I opened the door (I hated metal latch doors as I had seen too many horror films) I encountered a small step down into the very old and quirky bedroom with an en suite bathroom and a large imposing four poster bed which was somewhere that I had always wanted to stay in and now I was.

I could still feel the children around me as I started to unpack.

Lesley laid down on the right hand side of the bed to have five minutes shut eye before we went down for something to eat, as we were very hungry after the long journey. Suddenly she said,

"Feel the bed its freezing and I'm not imagining it" and it was as if a corpse was laying there already while my side of the bed was much warmer and quite comfortable. I intended to stick to my side thank you very much. This was strange as the cold area did not move at any stage and it really was like someone or something was already occupying that side of it.

Eventually both of us fell asleep for a few minutes (this was strange for me as you will see later) as we were shattered from our journey.

Hunger soon got the better of us and the smell of delicious hot food permeated through the building and with my keen nose I could smell steak and kidney pie so I had made up my mind what I was having before we reached the service counter. Orders placed, and with drinks in our hand we found a table to sit at as the Inn was quite busy at the time. I then did my usual trick of saying to Lesley would she swap seats as I felt uncomfortable where I was sitting and so we swapped - though you would have thought she would have learned her lesson by now. Anyway, our table number was called and I went to fetch the meals that where now ready to collect. We had both ordered the same food - steak and kidney pie with a puff pasty top, chips and vegetables and as I have said before, it smelt so good. The food was piping hot with steam emanating from the pies, then the chef said,

"You will need a towel as the plates are red hot" and they were, as no way could you pick them up without instant blisters.

As I returned to the table with the food I could feel both

plates burning my fingers so I hurriedly put the plates down and winced a bit from the finger pain and I wondered whether I had any fingerprints left. Then something very strange happened. As we began tucking into our food, which nearly burnt my mouth, Lesley pushed her meal towards me (feisty one that) and said,

'Its cold", I looked at her gob smacked and when I felt her plate it was cold and not just cold but chilled and it was then that I started to build up the impression of a tall man in a long cape standing behind her and I immediately told her as I always do.

Bless her she was so hungry I took her meal back and complained and the chef just laughed and said,

"He's always doing that it's just his thing" so he prepared her another meal and we moved tables where nothing more untoward happened, (Glad I swapped places originally though) call it instinct.

The food was good and on the way out we bumped into the owner and introduced ourselves and told him what we had come to do. I asked if we could do an investigation over the weekend and he was very accommodating and as the Inn was quiet we could have access to anywhere we liked and this was fabulous news. He would not come with us but could we write a report and give him copies of any photos that were of interest. Of course we could do this as these days you didn't have to wait for a chemist to develop them, which always seemed to take ages.

He was interested in the issue with the cold food and said,

"It is a common occurrence here but just take it back and get a fresh one" and laughed but Lesley didn't seem to find it amusing, but she could have said in hindsight that she didn't want to swap seats in the first place.

I felt the children around me as we went into the gift shop attached to the building and I was on the hunt for trigger objects (these are objects that can attract spirits or even be moved by them on occasions) and this shop was full of curiosities. We picked a small ball, a quill pen and we were just about to go to the counter when I noticed a large blue plastic pen with a clear plastic ball on top which when you pressed a button lit up a whirling field of bright colours. I had to pick up two of those as they felt right (I have carried these ever since on further investigations and they are now an integral part of my ghost hunting equipment replacing them with newer versions along the way) and suffice to say spirit children love then and are attracted to them.

I feel I was drawn to them by the two children (attachments) as I referred to them earlier.

We went for a walk around the grounds and took in the views across the moors, as it was a lovely sunny late afternoon now. I actually felt quite relaxed and safe now and possibly a few pints had contributed to that, if only I could have stuck with those thoughts as evening wore on I would become much the wiser.

Lesley and myself started our investigation quite early that first night in the kitchen, lounge, snug and bar areas but only a few orbs (these are spirit lights possibly the first stage manifestations of spirits or like the sceptics think dust, moisture, insects or anything else except paranormal) were caught on camera. Some like meteors were caught on the video night vision, which lit up the screen and some large ones on the digital still camera, which we asked spirit for, and got, but nothing really exceptional was captured. The room opposite us (apparently the most haunted on a regular basis was unoccupied and kindly the manager had opened it for us along with all the others on the top floor with the exception of one which was occupied) was the next area to be investigated but first we nipped into our room for a quick hot drink as it was getting cold now. We ended up staying in our room longer than expected as we turned the lights out as I had a hunch something was with us along with the children.

I was drawn to a chair at the side of the bed that did look rather old and worn but I was comfortable in it and that's what mattered and it also gave me a nice viewing angle of the bedroom and the bathroom door with the video camera. Lesley sat on the right hand side of the bed, which I must admit felt much warmer at this time.

I called out,

"If there are any spirits that wish to make themselves known to us please tap once for yes and twice for no,"

Nothing happened (funny that as from watching programmes on the television this should have worked instantly) and it never did and has never happened since to my knowledge.

Just as I was thinking what to do next the bed started to shake very lightly but it was visibly shaking and for no good reason and we were a little perturbed by this. Was this finally a spirit communication we were receiving as we sat in the dark very vulnerable and wondering what was coming next? Lesley got off the bed and went into the en-suite bathroom and I saw my opportunity to try a trigger object on the bed so out came one of the light pens and I pressed the button and it lit up the whole room for about a minute. I then placed it on the bed and invited spirit to come and investigate it, but some hope I thought to myself so I set the video night vision camera rolling and waited. I wasn't expecting anything to happen when probably one of the brightest orbs I have ever seen, came through the headboard then shot directly in the direction of the pen, hovered over it for a few seconds before moving off and disappearing through the wall to the side of me. This took me aback and I had caught it on film as well but nothing else happened in our room after that for a while so we moved to the room opposite - supposedly the most haunted in the Inn or on this corridor anyway. To say I was disappointed would be an understatement as except for a few orbs that could have been dust not like the orb acting intelligently in our room earlier nothing really happened. we ventured outside where the atmosphere was totally different and the wind coming off the moor was blowing the Inn sign making it creak even louder than usual it seemed. We snapped many digital photos and loads of orbs were caught with a majority being ruled out as anything to do with spirit, but one, half way along a dry stone wall, which was a watery blue colour, grabbed our attention. It looked like it had a face in it of a fairly young man (whenever I catch orbs now I always blow them up to see if there are any faces in them, a valuable tip as you may just recognise the person or animal portrayed in them) and as I was later to discover, a young man was sitting in that spot years ago before being lured onto the moor and was never heard of again, so this made the trip outside worthwhile.

It was getting late now. In fact we were well into the early hours of the morning when we decided to settle down for the night so we got ready for bed and Lesley was soon out like a light, which I could only dream, of as spirit seemed to steal her energy to pump into me to keep me awake so they could play and I would be left to face anything that they wanted to throw at me now. The word vulnerable comes to mind again.

If I went to sleep now, it would be with one eye open for sure. So I left the television on and the bedside lamp (big brave me).

Ten minutes went by with nothing but suddenly three large thumping bangs came from the en-suite bathroom, which resonated through to the bedroom and I was more than startled but I was not intending to investigate the source of those noises until the morning.

Nothing happened for quite a while until I noticed a bright golden orb floating around with a mind of its own. First left and then right up and down before heading towards the side of my bed and headed towards the bedside lamp. As it did, so the lamp dimmed down to a barely visible level and then the golden orb disappeared and the bulb returned to its usual level of brightness. I tried to wake Lesley but it was like trying to wake the dead, which probably would have been easier as I was finding out! This golden orb was not terrifying and gave me a similar feeling to my last night at the Halls of Residence where I wanted the apparitions to reappear as they fascinated me.

All went quiet again and I waited for something else to happen. I didn't have to wait too much longer.

Suddenly I could hear booted footsteps with buckles coming slowly along the corridor towards our room and then the one thing I dreaded - the gunmetal latch started to rattle violently as if someone was trying to come in. I didn't think to open the door and see who or what was there. I was just frozen to the spot and wished I was somewhere else. Lesley was still fast asleep over the other side of the large four-poster bed and I wished she would wake up but if I woke her up which would be the lesser of the two evils?, I've tried it before and its not recommended - trust me!

Suddenly the latch stopped rattling and the footsteps moved away soon becoming distant.

Now I had my brave head on and went and opened the door but I couldn't see anything anywhere that could have done that.

I was too scared to close my eyes now and prayed for the daylight to show itself so I could try and get some sleep at least.

Eventually it did as I noticed brightness appearing over the moor to my left and I felt I had earn't a reprieve - or had I?

Off went the television and the bedside lamp as I welcomed in the coming of the long awaited dawn announcing the start of a new day and no ghosts.

I settled down to try and get some sleep with my head under the covers when I felt as if something or someone was watching me but how could this be as ghosts only haunt at night or so I thought, how naïve of me.

I plucked up the courage to poke my head out from under the covers and found to my relief nothing was there and so with a sigh and a slightly raised heart rate I lay back down.

Then, all of a sudden, I felt cobwebbing moving across

my face and then down my back and it was icy cold. Suddenly the covers around my neck started to lift and slide gently off my body and down to my ankles in one movement. It couldn't have been Lesley as she was curled up in a foetal position and right across the other side of the bed and I couldn't even reach her. I pulled the covers back up, but that was it as I got out of bed, shaking and wishing I had eyes in the back of my head right now. I wished Lesley would wake up as I felt really alone and the temptation was to prod her but I thought better of it once again. I had had a totally sleepless night and felt like death warmed up right then and as I opened the bathroom door, fresh lumps of plaster were laying on the floor probably caused by the loud banging during the night but I didn't want to think about that right now.

That one night is something I can never explain and has had a profound effect on me becoming a serious ghost hunter, as I needed answers to all the events that took place that night. All I can tell you is, I went through every emotion that night and all I have relayed to you is true as it happened and don't forget, we still had another night to go yet in this remarkable place.

We went down to breakfast, which, by the way, was superb and nice and hot - including Lesley's and the proprietor asked if we had a good night and did we have any experiences (no I slept like a baby and had a wonderful night I thought to myself).

I told the proprietor about the incidents that had occurred overnight and the only thing that surprised him was the incident with the bedclothes being pulled off which apparently in his words were,

"That usually happens in the room opposite",

He then showed me a log of remarks left by people who had stayed at the Inn over the years and I was not surprised why he had not batted an eyelid as there were so many comments and surprisingly quite a few actually said,

"Disappointed as no ghosts came to visit", lucky them

who ever they were.

Later that day I was too tired to drive anywhere, so Lesley took the reigns and we headed for the coast on the route the smugglers would have used, hoping to pick up some trace elements. Nothing happened until we got to Polperro (by the way- it is beautiful and you could see why smugglers would use it). We walked down the narrow streets towards the beach and I had a feeling one of last night's uninvited guests had come along for the ride with us. It was a hot day with clear blue skies' full of circling seagulls, which were dive bombing unsuspecting folk as they were protecting their young. We sat down in a small café overlooking the bay when I heard the words,

"I'm Jack" which could only have come from this entity who was enjoying his day out with us.

Could he be the heavily booted man in the corridor from last night that rattled the door latch and put the fear of God in me? I will never know and after last night, nothing could faze me now and nothing has since - to that degree anyway.

I was becoming a hardened ghost hunter and it has lead me to many interesting and varied places over the years.

Back to Jack who was still hanging around with no intentions of going anywhere and he told me he had smuggled contraband for many years from here to London but eventually had been caught and found guilty of his crimes and as a result was sentenced to death and eventually hanged.

Then he was gone which brought me some relief and I really hoped that would be the end of him for the rest of the vacation.

The rest of the trip out was uneventful but I must say the scenery was breathtaking everywhere we went in Cornwall. If you've never been you must go, but spend a night at the Inn on the Moor along the way as its likely to be memorable.

On the way back near the Inn was a very old gaol that had seen many an execution so we decided to pay it a visit (we really are gluttons for punishment) as we were both really into ghost hunting now and still are. It was a very cold and desolate building with an eerie atmosphere and part ruined. At the time I wasn't really tuned into spirit, as I just wanted to see the place and relax a little after the previous nights experiences. As you walked around the cells you could see notices on the side telling you why certain individuals had been incarcerated and the punishments metered out to them.

Some were hanged for stealing a sheep or bread even (glad we didn't live in those times or did we, who knows really?) women included. Some were complete rogues and fully deserved what they got in my opinion, such as highwaymen, smugglers and murderers (what price a life in those days) who knew exactly what they were doing?

Lesley had her camera out and was on her usual orb hunt when I entered into a cell and I was pulled back violently by unseen hands. Lesley caught a massive orb in the middle of my back in a photo, so had a spirit guide pulled me back from a potential danger risk? I will never know, but it was very interesting.

Lesley in her own right, is a sensitive, but her forte is feeling the trauma that had taken the person from this earthly plain (lucky her) and glad its not one of mine. Spirit will show me how they died for validation for the recipient of the message. We were just coming to a rather negative looking staircase when she felt someone sever one of her arms. This shocked her as she had no feeling in her arm and she started to panic and was back up those stairs faster than a speeding bullet. When I eventually found her she was visibly shaking holding on to a nice hot latte (surprised she didn't spill it) and uttering what sounded like compete gibberish to me. She had full use of her limbs once again but did not want to investigate that place any further and of that she was adamant. I have been back but Lesley has stuck by her guns and never set foot in the place and never will again as it was probably her most paranormal experience to date and left a marked impression on her.

It is a strange place with a long and varied history and you know to treat it with resect when you enter into the courtyard and there in front of you is a trap door with a gallows standing above which makes you think. At least one of us was glad we took time to pay this somewhat disturbing, yet interesting place, a visit and there are so many places like this around the country.

Back to the Inn on the moor for a well earned dinner and hopefully a quiet night as I needed my sleep now.

We pulled up and the building looked as foreboding as ever but still held that fascination for me and I suddenly felt my attachments joining me and holding each of my hands. I was so used to them by now it felt comfortable (weird you may say but it is me you're talking too) and I think I would miss them if they didn't.

We made our way up to our room and noticed all the other rooms on the top floor were now occupied and this made me feel a little bit more secure and perhaps a less disturbed night was in store but who knew...

It was still broad daylight when we got back to our room and decided to have a quick nap. I actually slept and woke up an hour or so later feeling more refreshed and yes, I had actually slept. The atmosphere seemed to have changed and I felt more at ease, then we had a lovely dinner and I had a nice pint of cider to wash it down when we realised a ghost group had arrived and were occupying the vacant rooms. They asked us if we had experienced anything paranormal on the previous night and the proprietor winked at me from behind the bar and gave a wry smile. Should I tell all and spoil it for them? They obviously didn't have any psychics amongst them that was for sure. No I thought better of it and just said

"We heard a few bangs but they could have been anything". You may think that was a little bit mean but I was brought up a fisherman and the rule of thumb was you never told people what you had caught if you wanted to keep the best spot for yourself.

This place always seemed to change as the sun sank over the moor and lost its crimson glow. It's as if you could see the spirits walking across the moor to take refuge in the Inn for the night (my overactive imagination working overtime again) to do their bidding.

We reconvened in the bedroom to plan our attack for the night but things were getting noisy as the paranormal group laughed and giggled and drank more (nobody drinks on my vigils - it's a rule)) for Dutch Courage probably. I rang my Dad to tell him what had gone on the night before and that we didn't know what to expect from tonight. He seemed concerned and said,

"Pete no one will think any less of if you pack up and leave if you are worried" (he had had experiences in the past when he hadn't been looking for them but never disclosed the full detail of the facts),

I said "Its ok Dad. Last night just took me completely off guard and anything they throw at me now, I will be able to handle so see you when we get home".

The noises from the rabble in the corridors was intensifying and we decided not to investigate that night as we were both tired and had to travel to a guesthouse in Dorset the next day. We had definitely had enough evidence to prove the Inn was haunted beyond all reasonable doubt.

So now you are ready for another rollercoaster ride through the last night at the Inn on this occasion.

Hang on to your hollyhock's and I will tell you what happened next.

What happened next

Absolutely nothing (yes you heard me absolutely nothing) which surprised both of us big time.

Perhaps the noisy ghost hunting group scared the living daylights out of them or the spirits went off to tease them for the night but whatever it was we were left well alone, which I was rather grateful for. Though I never slept well at the Inn, I was so tired I actually dozed off a few times and felt quite refreshed by the time we woke up in the morning.

So a nice shower (as for some reason I would not sit in the bath with my back to the door as I felt I was being watched as happened in the haunted house I was brought up in), a change of clothes and down stairs for an amazing breakfast before we finally left for Devon. While sitting at the dining table in the bar area we noticed it was quite foggy outside and tendrils of wispy fog were coming in through the open windows like spooky arms. It was very atmospheric and something we have not experienced since and it was a nice way to finish our ghost hunt at the Inn - even if it wasn't paranormal.

What the ghost group caught during the night we never found out and it didn't really bother us as we had an experience we will never forget and myself especially.

Lesley was talking to the proprietor while I went upstairs to fetch the cases. As I went along the wonky corridor and into our room I felt I was being watched along with my regular attachments that did not want me to go, so I grabbed the bags and didn't hang around as I quickly evacuated the room and hastily retreated back downstairs to comparative safety. That Inn on the moor is an amazing place to stay and I would be back twice more over the next few years as it was now in my blood. We promised to write a full report for the proprietor and send him copies of the night vision videos and digital still pictures once they had been copied to disc and we were as good as our word like all good ghost hunters should, but often sadly don't in my experience.

As we left the Inn it was with a tinge of sadness as I now felt an attachment to it and not just through the two children, so goodbye until we were to meet again whenever that would be.

We had arranged to stay at a pub with bed and breakfast facilities in the Dorset village of Moreton on the way home. The village is the final resting place of Lawrence of Arabia whose remains are buried in the churchyard not far from the babbling river Frome. A crystal clear chalk stream with a head of wild brown trout in idyllic surroundings.

Lawrence's life came to such a tragic end in a motorcycle accident just outside the village of Moreton many years ago.

We booked into the Inn (another Inn) and decided to explore the surrounding area as it was only mid afternoon. It was hot and the birds were singing as we made our way to the church which is also renowned for being bombed in the blitz and having its stained glass windows blown out as a result. The windows were replaced with glass etched scenes depicting events of World War II including spitfires and Lancaster bombers etc. and well worth a visit if you ever find yourself in the area.

The graveyard is just across the road from the church where Lawrence of Arabia lies in peace and the reason I have put this in to the book was because Lesley found the following incident very funny.

As we neared the tomb of Lawrence we could see an American gentleman, as he was dressed in a cowboy hat, a shirt, shorts socks and sandals with the biggest domestic camcorder I have ever seen. This was a few years ago now and technology has advanced since then in leaps and bounds. He started recording and we thought that was that, but 10 minutes later he was still recording. Lesley nudged me with tears now rolling down her cheeks and had to hide behind a gravestone due to the uncontrollable fits of laughter emanating from her. Her words to me when she finally had enough control to speak were,

"What the hell does he think he's doing, and is he waiting for Lawrence to pop up and say hello or may be even sign an autograph or something", well enough was enough and we had to leave the area before we made bigger fools of ourselves.

A lovely story and memory we will both take to the grave and I hope you enjoyed it too.

After a lovely and very amusing afternoon we headed back to the Inn for a hopefully uneventful evening meal.

I was enjoying a steak and my usual pint of cider when I noticed a young lad in clothing not conducive with current times walk across the far side of the room and through the wall. He looked like a stable boy or farm hand and later I was to talk with the landlady who would tell me that where I had seen him disappear used to be a door long since bricked up through to the stables. Apparently he makes his presence known on a regular basis and went by the name of Tom. I didn't see him again during our overnight stay, which was a bit of a pity really.

While we were sat at the table the landlady came to us and said,

"There has been a mix up with the bookings and the only room we have left is the kids bedroom which is available as they are at boarding school", but we didn't really care, as all we needed was somewhere to lay our heads. We did quite well eventually as the bill showed we had only been charged for one person staying the night (there are good people out there and as a result we would be staying there again), which came as a surprise.

We climbed the carpeted stairs and passed framed photos of steam engines of all shapes and varieties along with other railway memorabilia. Then along a corridor and into the bedroom with two sets of bunk beds. That didn't bother me, but it was the clowns that seemed to be everywhere staring at you that had me on edge. It was like being in a circus with them hanging down from the ceiling, sat on shelves and even on the beds. Just what I needed right now and these kids seemed to have a morbid satisfaction for these sinister looking dummies and I rarely sleep well in strange places first night and these clowns really weren't going to help my cause.

Finally after a few more ciders for Dutch courage, I decided it was bedtime and with some trepidation I climbed the stairs alone as Lesley had already made her way up earlier on. Lesley was as usual fast asleep in the land of nod (how does she do that?) when we're in strange places and I wish I could unveil her secret.

Anyway I got ready for bed and turned out the lights but it was still fairly light in the room as there was a skylight in the ceiling and I could make out puppet like clowns plotting against me. I felt eyes boring into me from all directions and sleep seemed to be a distant dream at this time. I'm sure I saw a couple of them move (there goes my over active imagination again) and some looked to have swapped positions and were closing in around me. Then I must have fallen asleep as I was now so tired and all I remember is suddenly the face of queen Elizabeth 1st was right up close to mine and I leapt out of bed without removing the covers first. I swear I could hear the clowns laughing in unison all around me. I actually woke Lesley this time which was in itself an achievement and when I told her why her reply was,

"And your point is?" she knows me too well I'm afraid by now.

Nothing else happened but in the morning and as I was munching on my burnt toast as I had lost concentration through lack of sleep I couldn't help but wonder why had Elizabeth 1st paid me a visit.

Greece

After an eventful and wonderful break thanks to Lesley's birthday present to me, I just needed time to settle down and so it was back to work for the time being for both of us.

It wouldn't be long before our plans would change once again though, as while shopping in a small bustling town we went into the local travel agents and picked up a brochure for the Greek Islands.

We returned home and began to peruse through this very eye catching brochure and it was decided the Greek Islands where to be our destination but where? It seemed one place stood out to us and that was the picturesque island of Agistri two hours off the coast of Athens. The photos were beautiful if they were to be believed, so the decision was made and soon after the holiday was booked.

I thought to myself what if we were to make it into a honeymoon and it felt right and as we had already been engaged for what felt like an eternity I thought it was time to make an honest woman out of Lesley. I popped the question and was given a,

"Yes," which didn't really come as a surprise this far down the line.

The next few weeks flew by and we had a wonderful wedding at Leicester Registry Office and then a reception at my Mum and Dads house in Evington (no expense spared and I did the catering with some family help). It was a wonderful day (it doesn't have to be an expensive and all singing and dancing wedding to be very special) we will both never forget but all we wanted to do now was to get aboard the coach to London and Gatwick Airport.

The coach was full and nobody was prepared to move so that we could sit together and so we sat on opposite sides of the coach, which was fun when we wanted something to eat, pass the parcel with food came to mind.

Eventually, we reached the airport and we were on our

way to Athens. The plane touched down in the dead of night and as we came out of the plane it felt like I had just opened the oven door to check if the turkey was cooked (it was hot!). You know that familiar blast.

There were no ferries until the morning so we were whisked away by coach to a rest area where a continental breakfast was laid on. We could finally eat together some seventeen hours later.

A two-hour ferry ride to Agistri was the final leg of the journey which in total took all of twenty-one hours (what a way to spend your wedding night) and we were tired. The sun was now up and it was getting hotter as the ferry cruised into Agistri harbour leaving a trail of foam in its wake in the clear blue Aegean Sea. The scene was better than the glossy brochure had portrayed which is a very rare occurrence these days. It took our breath away as we sailed past white washed buildings towards a very small jetty flanked by pure golden sand and in the background where the pine clad mountains with the odd fluffy white cloud just making a token appearance. The harbour was a hive of activity with people rushing to and fro, everyone well versed in what they were doing. A small hill ran up to the narrow streets full of ramshackle houses and apartments. This was old world Greece make no mistake. We were loving it and we had only just arrived.

We settled down and felt blessed to have been guided to such a beautiful place because I believe that was what had happened. If we could imagine paradise it would probably be like this and the island was only seven miles around, so in two weeks we should be able to see most of it probably on a little moped. There were hidden secluded bays dotted all over the place to explore and fire tracks you could follow up into the mountains with the smell of pine hanging heavy in the air and where the sound of cicada beetles was deafening. On one day on a mountain fire track, I was in need of a drink and I had a bottle of water and as I unscrewed the top before it reached my lips I was surrounded by hundreds of thirsty wasps and where they came from so quickly I will never know but I threw the bottle away which was immediately pounced upon by the swarm and I feel I was rather lucky or my Guardian Angel was looking after me (so just a word of warning when drinking water in very arid areas especially pine forests - watch out for wasps) as we both could have been badly stung.

Now you are thinking when is something strange going to happen as it usually does where I'm concerned, but be patient as this island was so beautiful I had to sing its praises first.

It did but over the course of two holidays to this wonderful island.

We would recommend anyone looking for a fairly peaceful holiday in beautiful surroundings to stay here if you have the stamina to reach it in the first place.

One day while walking through the town there was a bright and colourful procession weaving its way through the narrow streets until we realised it was a funeral (now that's how you do a funeral). We had really thought it was a celebration and not a sombre occasion like this (a bit New Orleans style). We paid our respects by blessing the assembled party and made our way to the beach as we had really been looking forward to our honeymoon and we still had a few days to go yet and really couldn't bear the thought of having to leave this island which was like paradise to us.

In the afternoon as we walked along a dusty road with tumbleweed blowing along it when we passed some donkeys in a field and one of those donkeys was responsible for a child losing two fingers while trying to feed it during our holiday even though there was a sign reading in various languages,

"Don't feed the donkeys."

Anyway we came upon a group of houses all with their front doors wide open as was the island tradition and they allowed you to wander in at will and have a look around and many had soft drinks just inside the door and you could leave a donation, which we felt was lovely. Just then we were taken by the arms by two Greek folk and ushered into a house where many people had gathered for the wake of the person whose funeral we had witnessed earlier in the day. We went inside and were given a large glass of ouzo each and were asked many questions by the locals (more like a friendly interrogation really) as to where we were from and what we thought of their island. The house was full of icons shining copper and gold as the sunlight streamed through the windows. It had a strong smell of cigarette smoke and it was getting into my eyes and by rubbing them the sun cream on my face had managed to find its way into them and they were now streaming, so we said our goodbyes and left through the open door. My eyes were starting to focus again when I noticed propped up against the side of the house was a bright shiny coffin and I said to Lesley,

"How nice is that" until we walked past it and found a little old man standing in it not long departed this earthly plane.

I freaked out as I had never seen a dead person before but to Lesley it was old hat as being a nurse she would lay dead bodies out on a regular basis. That was a baptism of fire for me even though I had seen spirits since, as you already know a very early age.

Thinking back now what a lovely way to say goodbye to a loved one by inviting them to their own wake, these islanders had some funny customs.

The holiday came too an end and all too soon we were back in Leicester as a married couple with our honeymoon memories still fresh in our minds.

I will jump four years now to compete this series of events as I'm sure you don't want to wait.

We both loved our honeymoon on Agisti so much that we decided to return as it was calling us once again.

Back to the travel agents once again and we were booked for the same two weeks four years later in beautiful Agistri and we couldn't wait. We just hoped it hadn't changed too much.

The time to leave soon came and we were both excited, as we knew what to except from this holiday in what we had adopted as 'our little island'.

Off we went on the long excursion to our little Greek Isle and on our arrival we found the place had changed very little and as we walked into a taverna on the island, the first thing the Greek lady owner said was,

"You've been here before and its lovely to see you again" and then she proceeded to pour us a couple of drinks on the house.

That's what the locals are like on this little gem of an island in the sun and the food was as good as usual everywhere on the island, beef stiffado, chicken with pine nuts and lamb lemon before we even considered the plethora of seafood brought in fresh to the harbour side on a daily basis.

It made a change from fish and chips, burgers and pizza's back home (when in Greece eat like Greeks is my motto).

We were in our element here as before and we could relax for a couple of weeks in the sun and have some fun. The sea was as clear as a crystal and a deep azure colour and on one boat trip around the twelve islands we had dolphins running with the boat which was a very spiritual experience and left all aboard feeling humbled in a way only dolphins can make you feel. After the event everybody was talking to each other, which wasn't the case before these beautiful mammals arrived in our presence.

Another incident which I have to share with you before we get down to the interesting stuff was when Lesley and I were playing water tennis, which in itself was unusual as Lesley doesn't like being in the sea at all. I had noticed a small jellyfish bobbing about in the waves and I shouted to her,

" There's a jellyfish so be careful" and her reply took me rather by surprise

"I know what a bloody jellyfish looks like"

So with her wide knowledge on jellyfish we played on until a scream rang out as the jellyfish had stung her on the top of her leg. I dragged her out of the sea and her leg was already the size of a balloon and immediately found some ice to put on it to calm the pain but nothing seemed to work. There was no other alternative but to head for the local pharmacy that was hidden in a back street. When we eventually found it a very Greek chemist who did not speak a word of English met us, and I thought to myself this is going to be difficult as he just looked at us blankly and shrugged his shoulders. I grabbed a piece of paper and a pen and drew my best impression of a jellyfish and suddenly he uttered "ah mosquito" we were getting nowhere and after a frantic game of charades eventually he just waddled off and then came back with a tube of cream probably for piles or something else (I think he just wanted rid of us now as it was siesta time). Quite a few drachma lighter I left the shop with the wounded soldier limping along behind. We found a bench and I rubbed the miracle cream into the top of her leg and very soon the swelling seemed to start to reduce and the pain subsided slowly. I don't think Lesley has swum in the sea since that incident and I don't think she ever will. I tried to get her a book on salt-water invertebrates being the kind and dedicated husband I am but they were all in Greek I'm afraid.

I had to put that little story in as it's my autobiography and it still makes me laugh today so I hope you enjoyed it too.

A couple of days later still quite early in the morning but it was as hot as hell already, we ventured down the dusty street towards the local bakery for some supplies. It was busy with locals going to work and holiday makers heading for the beaches when I noticed a Greek man dressed like a fisherman walking straight towards us and he wasn't moving out of the way anytime soon. As he reached us I pushed Lesley out of the way who promptly said,

"What did you do that for" (polite for her after yesterday's events) "So that bloke didn't knock you over" I said

"What bloke" she retorted.

I said "The fisherman in the smock and wellingtons"

She said "there was no man that looked like that, go and have a look for yourself," so I did and I searched high and low in the bakery and dragging Lesley with me down the side streets but he was nowhere to be found. There was nowhere he could have gone and there weren't any houses nearby with open doors but he felt as real as you and I. Had I had a run in with a real ghost, I began to ponder that thought process, and as we headed to a taverna for breakfast and a cup of coffee, I still couldn't get my head around this incident and it was really starting to bug me now and I needed some answers. We left the taverna and were heading back to the hotel when Lesley said,

"We need to head to the money exchange before they close,"

So we made a detour to the exchange and waited to be served standing as close to the air conditioning as we could get to try and keep cool as it was scorching outside now. We knew the guy at the exchange as he was also connected with the hotel where we were staying,

He said, "How are things going"

I replied, "Were having a great time as always and the people are so nice here,"

He said, "That's how we try to be here," and smiled,

I then asked him,

"There was an incident this morning where a man seemed to walk into us so I pushed Lesley out of the way but she said there was no one there,"

He seemed very interested at this point and then asked,

"What was he dressed like"?

I said, "He looked like a typical Greek fisherman with a smock and wellingtons but he was very weather beaten looking with a thick moustache and I never found him again"

The man in the exchange then asked suddenly,

"What's the date today" with a puzzled look on his brow, and then he smiled and said,

"I know who you have seen"

" Who" I asked,

He replied, "He was the skipper of a local fishing boat who passed from a massive heart attack while at sea. There was a huge procession for him four years ago today as he was such a popular figure and a big part of the island". His widow lives in the big house at the top of the road next to the donkey field."

You could have knocked me down with a feather when I realised that

it was the same house that we had been invited into for a glass of ouzo four years ago to the day and the Greek man stood up in the coffin was only the same fisherman I had run into earlier in the day.

I had seen a ghost and I could prove it with good validation and I was pumped up with various emotions.

The man in the exchange offered to take me up to meet the old fisherman's widow but I declined his offer as it was all new to me then but if it had been now as I write this I would jump at the chance.

It was an amazing experience and really the start of my awakening to talk to spirit.

The rest of the holiday was pretty uneventful regarding ghosts but we still had a wonderful time as ever.

A very busy time ahead

I now take you back a few years as I wanted to tell you the Greek series of events as one big chapter and I hope you enjoyed it and

little things had now started to happen gradually which I will try to remember as best I can.

I wanted to go fly-fishing for trout on a local reservoir one weekend and had arranged to meet with my friend Dennis at an old little pub in our village. I got there early so I sat on a stool at the bar in the snug and waited. Dennis was never one for punctuality and usually showed up late, but his character made up for that.

This particular night was no different but I had my back to the swing door and was minding my own business and I was talking to the landlord when after about twenty minutes I heard the swing door open and then felt a slap on my backside which was not Dennis's usual greeting and a great big hand slapped down on my shoulder.

I said,

"About bloody time mate where the hell have you been" but there was no reply and I got the impression of a large man standing beside me who resembled an old worker from the local quarry and then he was gone.

I turned to the landlord and asked him

"Is this place haunted"?

He replied" Why do you ask? "

I said "Because someone has just slapped me on the bum and put his hand on my shoulder"

He said, "That's old George from the quarry up the road he comes in here regularly and he was one for the lads" and laughed.

So another visitation with validation to back it up and this was becoming more common these days, I had never heard this story before but I knew it was true now.

Dennis did turn up eventually and I was quite glad to see him and we did have a good days trout fishing and a good laugh about George the next day on the boat and may have nearly fallen in at times.

I was now really getting interested in the world of the paranormal but at this time any thoughts of being a medium were furthest from my mind.

I had heard on the grapevine about a local paranormal group in my area so I started the process of hunting them down (pardon the pun) and eventually caught up with them in a large pub not too far from my village. This is meant to be, I thought, to myself and it seemed to appear to be the case.

I met with the group a few times and really enjoyed it and we hunted in supposedly haunted local venues and were quite often seen wandering about graveyards in the countryside during the dead of night. This was all well and good but I felt we could do more bigger and exciting venues. At the time I was working in the Pest Control business which gave you access to places that some could only dream of being allowed into. Lets face it - everybody has to have pest issues at sometime whether it be a castle, a pub, a railway engine shed and even a mansion house so I was an asset to have on their team and I did come up with the goods.

I would talk to some clients about the possibility of carrying out a ghost hunt on their premises and rarely got rebuffed. At other times I would see something that would make me ask questions to the owners and they would get interested and offer the venue to me for us to investigate. Sometimes I actually saw ghosts on the premises and when the owners validated the sighting we were in.

One such Leicester nightclub venue called me out as they had sighted mice upstairs and I went up to solve their problem.

I rang the doorbell and it was answered almost immediately by a young manager who told me he was the only one working at that time and to help myself.

This was the usual case in most venues I went to as much of my job was down to trust and once I had gained access I had a look around the ground floor but nothing of any significance was found. As I climbed the staircase to the upper level a young girl walked straight across in front of me without glancing back and headed towards the double fire exit doors and as I reached the top of the staircase,

I shouted,

"Hi, I thought there was only one person working today" but there was no reply just dead silence (more puns) greeted my question,

I ran downstairs and spoke to the young manager about him not being alone and he assured me he was and then he said,

"Wait a minute a young girl has been seen recently by different members of the staff and public on the upper level and I'm starting to suspect we have a ghost".

After I had finished my mouse inspection and found the culprit was a biodegradable bag, which had shredded with time under the bar I asked the young manager if there was any chance of doing a ghost hunt at the venue sometime and I was quite surprised when he said, "Yes I don't think that would be a problem".

So I left the premises and started to draw up plans for a future investigation. I had suggested that a Sunday would be best as the club would be closed and we could start late afternoon and be finished before midnight as we all had work to go to the following morning.

Two weeks later at three o'clock on the Sunday afternoon we started our investigation (it doesn't have to be dark to ghost hunt as most people think) downstairs. Some of the group went straight for the 'dead board' much too my horror but I watched from a distance as that thing was still my nemesis. They seemed to be in communication with a woman who had practiced the dark arts many years previous and that was enough for me and so I wandered off somewhere else as I knew what that instrument was capable of.

It was getting dark outside but the building had very

little light coming in anyway so it felt very atmospheric when I first picked up on an old man who had very dirty hands, wore goggles and an old leather apron so he had to be from a time previous to the night club (I hoped) anyway. He gave me the impression he was standing over a press but he felt like a kind hearted old chap who would have loved his job. It turned out later that many years ago the building was the printing site of the local Leicester newspaper so it finally all made sense to me. Then, a few minutes later, up on the first floor, I noted another set of stairs up to a very large attic and so I started to climb them to investigate this area. One of the crew was taking photographs on the first floor and was near the foot of these stairs when I felt a massive energy surrounding me and I shouted out,

"Quick take a picture there's something with me"

The crewmember duly obliged, and what was caught on the photo was truly amazing,

Now one of the rules of our investigations was nobody was allowed to smoke due to possibly of contaminating any evidence we may capture and it was always a fire risk so there was a safe area down on the ground floor where you could relax, chat, eat and drink which I think was pretty fair on everybody.

The crew member said

"Pete come and take look at this"

I went back down the stairs and the picture instantly blew me away.

I was standing near the top of the stairs with a mist enveloping me in the shape of a dragon like creature with a big eye, which was wrapping itself around me. I was speechless but totally fascinated as I didn't feel this energy was in anyway negative.

It was a photo that would lead me on my spiritual journey in the years to come (many have seen the photo and have no explanation for it) but I did not realise this at the time.

I was really excited now and walking around with my

night vision video camera I started to ask out to spirits to show themselves. I was fast becoming a ghost hunter with a real thirst for the truth.

Down one of the corridors were some staff quarters and as I asked out orbs would be seen spinning and moving on command and when the crew took photos of us I would seem to be the one with orbs attached to me, but why me?

We never did get any communication with the young girl I had seen on the first floor while working, perhaps she was happy doing what she was doing and I had no problem with that but it would have been nice to find out who she really was.

Nothing else really happened and by ten o'clock we were ready to call it a night as the working week loomed which was never nice.

We said our goodbyes until the next time we met up at the usual public house.

I was hungry for more and it wasn't long before another investigation fell into my lap and this was to happen many times more and still continues to the present day.

I was working in a very old notorious public house in Leicester and I was down in the cellar, I had my workbag propped against the door at the top of the cellar steps as I hated it down there for some reason (call it my intuition) when I heard a grating sound and noticed a beer barrel rolling slowly across the floor at the far end of the cellar so I was out of there rather more quickly than I had anticipated. As I came up the steps a violent thunderstorm was raging outside and the pub looked very dark and sinister now, as the patrons had all gone home. Then I heard a thoroughly evil voice utter the words

"Get out"

I didn't need a second invitation and left that area, and I felt this needed investigating but not on my own and I casually asked the landlady,

"Would it be possible to investigate the pub one night"

Her reply was "Yes love when would you like to

come," another one that came to me out of the blue.

Arrangements made we all arrived on the night about eleven o'clock as the punters would all have gone home by then.

It was the usual crew with a few added guests who had asked to join us that were going to experience an interesting night.

We started in the cellar and orbs were caught which may have been drain flies but not the banging coming from somewhere in the dark at the far end of the cellar. It was getting colder as I started to build up the impression of a tall woman in a shawl and a veil standing in front of me but as only I could see her I put it down to over active imagination once again and it was as if we were in her space and we needed to leave so I asked out, as I was confident doing this now,

"If there are any spirits here who wish to make contact please do so now" (I knew there was),

"Can you touch one of us, move an object or throw something,". A scraping sound at the far end of the cellar similar to what I had heard on the previous visit, and then something metal crashed into one of the barrels and seemed to be thrown with some force I may add. It took us all by surprise and very quickly we were back in the pool room, I think without touching a single step on the way back (such brave souls) to catch our breath. Two of us finally descended the steps with torches on to try and find what had been thrown and there on the floor near where the impact was heard could be seen a coin. It was a nineteen forty-five silver shilling and we were amazed (the landlady still has it to this day and still proudly shows it off to people), but where had that come from and why that item in particular.

We were back in the bar now and sitting quietly when we all heard a bell ringing somewhere nearby in the pitch black and as a torch was switched on and pointed in that direction. We could see it was the patron's bell that hung down from the shelf where the pint glasses were stored and it was ringing by itself with nobody near it.

Later we were in the corridor connecting the toilets and trying to make communication with spirit when the toilet door opened and I expected some one to come out but nobody did.

I was using night vision in the corridor and I kept catching one persistent orb flying around which did not leave the corridor and seemed to have a fascination with the camera and wanted to talk (this was not a piece of dust by any stretch of the imagination) to us.

I had an EVP machine running sat on the carpet in the corridor (for those who don't know what that is, it's an electronic voice phenomena machine which can capture spirit voices and messages), which would capture a first class voice recording in this corridor when played back the next day.

I asked out "Can you tell us what is your name" (knowing full well the name it should be from the history of the site).

The reply from spirit was crystal clear,

"I'm Mary"

Mary was the ghost most associated with the history of this site and used to live in the cellar with her children, which was why she did not like people down there invading her space.

The outside garage used to be a building where bodies were stored after hangings at the nearby gallows and this was to be the last investigation of the night.

We all filed into the garage and shut the doors and turned the lights out as you do and different people experienced being touched and one person was pushed which resulted in a few customary screams along the way. All I could see was a huge dog with red eyes staring at us (hopefully it was my over active imagination working overtime) and I called an end to the vigil before things could get nasty.

The next interesting vigil was one arranged by others in the group and not myself this time and was to be the beginning of the end as far as my association with this team went.

It was a night visit to an old abbey ruins in Leicestershire (which I have been back to many times since and even walk the dogs there occasionally).

It was still light when we arrived at the ruins and it looked ok in the evening glow. The ruins were silhouetted against the darkening skies with the rough granite sticking out in various directions and in places piercing the sky. Rooks were circling above the stonework before heading to the nearby rookery for the night and it was getting dark as we headed down the wooded path towards the abbey. Bats were dive-bombing us now and owls hooted in the distance as the last fingers of light were being eaten up by the black of night. When we first got out of the car I felt the energy of a nun around me who seemed to insist on staying with me for the visit.

We walked past the field where henry VIII's men had camped the nights before the dissolution of this abbey. Photos were taken and many orbs were caught and got the guests very excited and I must admit some were interesting me and warranted further investigation. Then on through the gloomy glen which it was by now and you could not see your hand in front of your face.

Crunching over rocks and rubble by torchlight we reached the ruins and within minutes people were catching strange mists and light anomalies all over the place. I still had this energy with me and to prove it I was tested with a K II meter, which lit up like a Christmas tree with flashing coloured lights everywhere (KII is a meter that lights up when electric magnetic frequencies are recorded which is what ghosts and spirits are supposed to be made up of) which left folk in no doubt that something was there as there are not any electrical cables or power points in the old ruins. People found it fascinating and all the other meters were dead until they were placed in my vicinity at this time. Some of the group went off and did their own thing and some stayed with me.

I was being drawn to the old ruined chapel when somebody asked me if I could get a name for this nun.

I had never done anything like that before but I cleared my mind and subconsciously asked the nun her name. Into my head came a name and I said "Rosita", but I wasn't comfortable with that for some unknown reason.

I tried again and this time much clearer I said the name,

"Rosia" not a name I was familiar with anyway and then we all heard a little giggle followed suddenly by a stone hitting the wall of the chapel very delicately and fell at our feet.

I said "Rosia if that's you can you throw another stone" then another was picked up and thrown as if in a game and this happened a few more times and then stopped as quickly as it had started.

I thought to myself how did I get that name, I'm not a medium and anyway they are bunch of charlatans who trick people out of money for personal gain (I was the worlds biggest sceptic which you probably find strange reading about my life so far) and I apologise if that statement has upset many of my friends. I have had to eat my words in recent years and now believe true mediums are a valuable piece of the puzzle regarding the after life and I bow to you all with great reverence.

I was beginning to realise I had abilities I really did not understand and I needed to learn more but how I just did not know at this time.

Back to the vigil and after the amazing stone throwing incident, things seemed to calm down and I went in search of part of the crew that had me a little worried with good reason. I found them sitting and chanting something in a little group at what looked like a stone altar and when I arrived they put something away hurriedly and quickly dispersed. They were up to no good of this I was sure and the dark arts were involved I felt and the more vigils I did with them the worse they got confronting and abusing spirit (remember spirit were once like we are now and should be respected as such) and I was getting more than a bit worried. The rest of the vigil went without a hitch and some people got photos that they still keep now and they seemed to have had a good night. Rosia the nun stayed with me until we got back to the car park where I thanked her for her help, then blessed her and instantly the lights went out on the KII and she was gone.

Everybody accounted for, we all departed for the night and it wasn't until the next afternoon I got a phone call from one of the group who had been researching the previous nights events with the aid of the Internet. He had come across an article about a nun at the abbey who was known as Rosia, You may say I read it up on the internet before I went, but I never do on any investigation as I now let spirit guide me but what could I gain from making it up, well absolutely nothing.

Out with Old and In with the New

The group had managed to get a vigil in a hall on a park in Leicester, which had a reputation for ghosts and strange goings on.

I had a feeling this would be my last vigil with the group and it was to be just the case.

We parked at the rear of the hall which looked very imposing with a sinister looking tree with a massive branch hanging off it, which I felt someone had been hanged from (I hate being right as I found out later) through a gut feeling.

We went inside and the building was enormous with copious rooms and massive sweeping staircases.

Lesley and myself would go off on our own eventually so we didn't get mixed up in anything dark but we decided to go to the massive cellar first where the dark arts had been practiced over the years and was supposed to be heavily active, paranormally, along with everyone else.

Once in the cellar a hand holding séance was carried out by a medium the group had brought in (I wasn't a medium) to liven things up a bit. Within minutes he was stomping around the cellar talking in riddles and stating he wanted to stay down there. Remember I was still slightly sceptic and found this amusing until he picked up a stick from the cellar floor and stood in the middle of the séance with it and I noticed it changing into a sacrificial dagger with a curled snake on the shaft which freaked me a bit. It was passed around the group but nobody could see what I could see until it was passed to Lesley who dropped it like a hot coal and dismantled the séance in one fell swoop. When I caught up with her I asked her what was wrong and she had seen what I had seen and that's why she dropped it. How very strange we had both seen the same thing.

After that incident we went off on our own and it wasn't the wisest decision we have ever made, the pair of us.

Screams and shouts were coming from other areas of the big house, and some pretty unrepeatable I may add, but we were happy on our own little vigil. We firstly went down to the classroom area, which immediately brought scenes from the war to my mind like Churchill's bunkers and army personnel leaning over a table to plan a strategy. No communication was forthcoming so this was probably a residual haunting or stone tape theory where the buildings hold memories of the past and replay a scene - which is totally different to the ghost with an attitude I was soon to meet, who left a marked impression on me - quite literally.

We were walking around the ground floor and passed through a large room when I picked up on the energy of an artist with his pallet of oil paints. He was very brash and self opionated so I tried to block him out but he had a strong energy and I turned to Lesley and said

"I have an artist here and he thinks he is the dog's crown jewels of artists," (or words to that effect) which was a big mistake in hindsight. He kicked me square on the shin and I felt it and soon my left shin was very painful. I rolled up my trouser leg and there was a bruise like a duck egg with a trickle of blood weeping from it. Lesley was shocked, as she knew I hadn't bumped into anything and had been with me constantly. This is what some describe as a psychic attack and is something that can happen when ghosts get wound up - so be warned that this can happen. That bruise and cut did not heal up for six weeks, which was very strange. I was not enjoying this particular vigil and felt I had different ideas of how a ghost hunt should be run and as I look back now I was right. Just before two o'clock in the morning the fire alarms went off and it was not spirit orientated but some of the local youth who knew we were in the hall and thought it would be funny to set fire to some junk mail and post it through the letter boxes at the front and back of the building. Obviously they had started various fires but luckily the halls alarm system was linked to the fire station and soon two units arrived to put them out and the police also turned up. They arrested some of the youths and the fires were put out but after a very important discussion with the police it was decided to terminate the ghost hunt with immediate effect. We were very glad about that personally and as the police could not guarantee our safety or our vehicles for the rest of the night that was it for us and with the group as a whole.

We could have died in there that night through some idiots' stupidity so please be careful and choose your venues carefully.

I had had an idea of going freelance as a ghost hunter and this was now my chance and I was going to grab it with both hands but as for communicating with spirit the thought had never really entered my head but that was about to change too.

I think back now to a strange conversation I had with Mum many years ago.

Mum had taken me into town with her to collect a lamp she had ordered a few weeks previously (no internet or on line shopping in those days) and really just to have a trip out together as we usually went everywhere as a family (yes that happened in those days as well) so these occasions were special. I was the youngest of three and there was a reasonable age gap between my brother, my sister and myself and I often felt a bit left out.

We arrived at the shop and the assistant carefully took the lamp out of its two boxes to check it over. It had the wow factor from the first moment I laid eyes on it. It was made of cut Waterford Crystal Glass both the base and the lampshade and that's why it came in two boxes and the myriad of colours and the prisms it gave off were a sight to behold.

I said, "Mum its beautiful"

She replied, "That's why I brought you along as one day it will be yours". I was ecstatic at the thought that one day this beautiful item would be in my possession. True to her word, many years later the lamp takes pride of place in our house still giving off its radiant colours. Then she said to me straight out,

"Now listen son, I have this gift I'm afraid to use as it scares me. You have the same ability but I feel you will be able to handle it as you grow older"

I hadn't grasped what she was on about really and then Mum continued,

"You know you see people that are no longer here (that was a very polite way of putting it I felt) as you have proved to me many times already and this will only get stronger as you gain more knowledge"

"When I die I will help you learn to control it, but don't tell your father about this little chat as he would not understand"

Mum religiously went to church on Sundays with Dad and invariably the three of us kids as well, so I was now very mixed up about all this.

She kept her word and once she had passed to spirit, things started to gather pace as you will see later.

She had gone into hospital for a hip replacement and during the operation had a stroke, which she survived. Unfortunately, life was never the same for her, and Dad became her carer in the end. Her condition worsened over a short period of time until early one morning she passed away and I was devastated along with the rest of the family.

It was still dark when she passed and my Dad and sister were with her at the time. The rest of the family had visited the day before, myself included, and we knew the crossing over would not be long away and soon my sister rang around everyone to say,

"Mum passed peacefully in the early hours" and it was a blessing really and I think everybody inwardly thought the same really including Dad if truth be known.

The strange thing was my brother rang me very early on the day and it was still pitch black as none of us could sleep. He said they had a robin singing outside their bedroom window for about twenty minutes a little earlier. This was ironic as when he rang we had been listening to a robin singing in the garden for about the same period of time (I am now a great believer in Mother Nature allowing spirit to use her creatures as spirit messengers after many unexplainable incidents in recent years) and that was more than a coincidence.

Probably ten minutes before the sad and final phone call, Lesley had said she felt her lips being softly kissed and a strong smell of violets. This did not surprise me one bit as Mum's last request was to die with dignity at home though the doctor was insistent she had to go into hospital and after a massive argument, which none of the family needed, and the Doctor not listening the ambulance turned up (I don't think Mum would have even made it to hospital) and the crew recognised Lesley straight away and saw how distraught she was.

Lesley was a nurse and very highly thought of within the profession and still is to this day. After a few minutes conversation between the crew, Lesley and the doctor, it was finally decided to let Mum have her request and die with dignity in her own home surroundings for which we will be forever grateful and I am not surprised Mum personally thanked her.

Mum had said a few weeks before she passed to spirit, that she wanted to take her little Yorkshire Terrier 'Scampi' with her as Dad would have enough to cope with once she had crossed over which was a bit of a strange thing to say.

Never a truer word was spoken only a few weeks later while

Dad was trying to get on with life and we all stayed very close to him as I don't think he believed that Mum was actually going to die, though we could all see it but he was too close. A very familiar scenario to many I suspect,

It was a routine weekday morning shopping trip on foot down to the local village shops with Scampi trotting along beside him and as he got near the shops he could see a very large Alsatian dog, which had a well known bad reputation in the area, tied up outside a convenience store on a piece of rope. It saw little Scampi, broke it's rope and attacked the little dog tearing into it and tossing it in the air like a rag doll. When the dog finally let go Scampi was in a very bad shape and Dad was in a state of shock just clutching onto Scampi in a futile attempt to save her, but she died in his arms. Dad really didn't need this at eighty-five years of age and just having lost his wife a couple of weeks previous you would not wish that on your worst enemy.

What of the Alsatian, I hear you ask? Well it was finally found by the police and destroyed, but funnily enough, a medium brought my Mum through a few years ago and she has two dogs with her, one a little Yorkshire Terrier and the other a great big Alsatian. I will let you decide.

I was excited about becoming a paranormal investigator in my own right and couldn't wait to get out and about and it wasn't long before my brother rang to see if I would go with him to a local Guildhall for a trip out and I eagerly agreed. I thought this could be fun and rang the medium that worked with the group I had just left and he agreed and all three of us met up even though it was during the day and not at night when most ghost hunts take place. It wasn't really an investigation but more a visit to see what we could pick up on and try and verify what we had found. We started in the café as on most day visits anywhere we usually do and I'm sure cafes are strategically placed near the entry and exit points for that reason.

We started in a very old part of the building and very soon I began to build up impressions of people not of this time who had now joined with us. Our invited guest was in a trance like state and shouting out names and was supposedly, having conversations with ghosts that I was having a problem seeing but he was the medium so we went with it. I picked up on a very rotund looking chap in a very old uniform with a ruddy complexion who had a large bunch of keys on his belt, who was walking down a narrow staircase (trust me he only just fitted) I was standing at the bottom of. Why was our medium friend not picking up on him I thought to myself, anymore real and you could trip over him! I inwardly chuckled.

He was later verified as one of the original police force, which started here and was a very well known character in the Guildhall's history. We moved on to the underground cells which were very atmospheric and I felt eyes watching me when our medium invited me to stay in one of the cells on my own for a few minutes while he carried out some kind of incantation. I wasn't going to be used as a guinea pig for nobody, so I flatly refused - much to his disappointment. Call it intuition but it wasn't going to happen and to this day I don't do lone vigils and I don't expect any of our guests to do so either.

At one point in the cellars we did catch a large bright orb on video camera, which zoomed between the medium and myself but turned out to be my spirit helper and guardian angel, as I would find out at a later date. As we left this area we passed an iron maiden (an iron cage in the shape of a human body which criminals were crammed into as a means of torture), which was hanging up. Our medium for the day invited it to swing and it started to do so slowly and then more quickly which was quite impressive I thought, as it was a heavy object.

We moved to another area, a large room with paintings on the wall and with plush furnishings where I started to get the impression of a tall man with a goatee beard, long black tunic, dark hair and a black cloth cap on his head, when my brother said,

"Carry on - what else can you get,"

I thought my brother recognised him or something and then he said

"He is standing behind you, just turn around" I thought he had lost it for a minute so I turned round but still could not see anything.

"The painting on the wall behind you" he said and sure

enough there was the same man as I had seen smiling down at me. I was shocked as I hadn't even been over that side of the room.

Then something very strange happened which has had a great bearing on my spiritual development.

All three of us were still in this same room when a very smartly dressed lady who must have been in her forties and well spoken came up to me and said,

"You're a medium aren't you," to which I replied,

"No, but the chap over there is though" then she said,

"No its you I am talking too as when I am around mediums I get strange vibes like a rush of electricity and trust me you are one," and you could have knocked my brother and myself down with a feather.

This perfect stranger had just come up to me and called me a medium now this was exciting news.

I chatted with this lady for a while before her husband dragged her off, as he was probably as big a sceptic as myself at that time. How strange I thought, as she seemed so determined to get her message across to me. I would love to meet her again and thank her for helping me change my life. If you ever read this book, you will know who you are. Please get in touch.

Our medium friend had to go soon after, leaving my brother and myself to finish the tour on our own.

One more strange thing happened which was when I saw the image of a dog over by a lectern in another large room and it looked very much like a lurcher to me, so we both went to investigate further and my brother was only too delighted to go with anything I saw these days as it fascinated him also.

As we approached the lectern the sun was streaming through the window directly on to it and bathing it in a golden glow and as I climbed up, there to my surprise I could see in the thin layer of dust a large paw print and we were both amazed. Why I had to ask myself would a dogs paw print be clearly visible in an old Guildhall I will never know. Before we finished our visit we nipped back into the large room to take another look but the paw print had vanished as if it had never existed until we noticed on one of the paintings we had missed on the way round (you've guessed it there was a lurcher in one of them). How very strange. Back to the café as we had to pass it on the way out for a cup of tea, a bite to eat and a discussion on what had just happened.

We said our goodbyes and I made my way home alone with my thoughts and when I finally arrived home I felt rather drained which was unusual for me and soon fell asleep. Could it have been from spirit using my energy? I was soon to find out.

Lesley came in from work and I was still fast asleep on the couch but she did not disturb me and when I eventually stirred Lesley asked me if I'd had a good day,

"Yes" I said "but some really strange things happened" and I started to explain in great detail about all the sightings during our visit to the Guildhall. She had heard these things many times over the years from me until I mentioned the lady and what she had said. She suddenly seemed to take a lot more interest in the conversation.

Then she said" it doesn't surprise me as I've been saying for ages now there is something going on with you that's not normal (that's possibly many things if you know me well enough) and we need to sort it out," What could that mean I wondered to myself? Next thing I knew, Lesley had the laptop on and was searching for something on line which as it turned out, she was looking up meeting times for the local spiritualist churches and as it happened there was one in town meeting that night at seven thirty and I was going. No questions asked as she said,

"You need to meet with a medium" and you know my thoughts on mediums at that time, but after much protestation I lost and we decided to go.

We turned up at the church with half an hour to spare and sat out side in the foyer but I couldn't help but notice this big man staring at me. We waited for a while not knowing what to do next when this great big man headed towards us (I thought he was a bouncer and he going to kick us off the property) but what a surprise I got as he was one of the nicest people I had met in along time.

We stood up and he told us to sit down again and took my hand and smiled and then he spoke.

He told us his name and then said, "You need to see me as you have many questions that need answering," I thought "good guess - why else would we be here"?

Then he said" Spirit tells me you have three important questions that need answering at this time" and I had which shocked me a bit and I was running out of coincidences and was starting to take this bouncer seriously and what he said next blew me away,

"You had an unexpected conversation with a lady very recently that you can't get your head around," (only earlier today) and before I could reply he again said,

"You have a picture on you that you don't understand and you had an incident while on holiday that you can't figure out and I'm sure its your mother who has passed to spirit telling me this." Well those few words left me in awe of this big man as he turned out to be the medium running the open circle that night and everything he said was spot on and then he took my hand again and said words I will never forget.

"You can do exactly what I do as a medium but it has needed someone to tell you this at the right time which by the way is now and be prepared for a rapid increase in spiritual activity as now they know that you know and the last bit scared me a little and then he took Lesley's hand and said,

"Both of you work well together but you are the medium and your wife is your battery pack" (I thought back to the times Lesley had fallen asleep in certain Inns for no apparent reason and I was so pumped up that sleep was not on the agenda and it seemed to make sense now) as we weren't on a first name basis at this time.

The picture was the one in the nightclub, which I had brought with me, the incident was the one at the Inn on the moor when the bedclothes had been pulled off me and the lady was the one who spoke to me in the Guildhall,

Wow this guy was good and my scepticism had just received a massive dent.

He asked us if we would like to stay for the open circle and we decided to try it and why not, after all that's what we were there for.

As we walked into the main body of the church we noticed men and women sat on chairs casually dressed and chatting away and there wasn't a cassock or dog collar in sight and there was a lot to learn.

I felt comfortable as I sat down and started talking and that was when I met with Caroline Clare

Anyway, a prayer was said to thank the Divine Spirit for allowing us to meet safely tonight, and that spirit would aid us in speaking to our loved ones passed over.

Lesley and I were introduced to the group and I explained why I had come there that night and I thought people would say wow that's amazing but they just clapped once I had finished my somewhat strange tale as if it was a common series of events.

We did colour meditations, which I really enjoyed when the big man said to one of the group,

"Can you take Pete with you onto the stage and try and bring a message through from somebody's loved one in spirit between you.

I had never done something like this before and I felt very nervous with nowhere to hide right now. The young girl who was very good by the way started to describe a person who suddenly started to form in my subconscious at the same time and I carried on with the next bit and then we both carried on with descriptions until someone in the circle recognised who it was coming through and I remember we gave a lovely message for them. I had been seeing people like this for years but now it was all starting to make sense and the only thing I didn't realize was that they brought messages through with them.

We both got a massive round of applause and I was

really looking forward to the next time I could try this.

I was a welcome addition to the group along with Lesley (my battery pack) and could not wait for the next week.

On the way out Caroline grabbed me and said,

"Well done - that was impressive" and I made my way home with a spring in my step.

Perhaps if I had had an inkling of what was to happen that night I would not have rushed home so readily and with the big mans words still ringing in my ears we went to bed fairly early because we both had a full day of work ahead of us.

The lights went out and I snuggled down to sleep and things were fine until I heard my name called which woke me with a start.

The bedroom was dark with just a little light oozing into the room through a crack in the curtains from the outside streetlights.

I thought I saw a shadow move around the wall and then another and another and this was starting to worry me and for some reason I looked up and the ceiling seemed to have been replaced by a balcony with faces of all shapes and descriptions looking down and calling to me. I had no idea how to control or stop this from happening when I noticed a young girl skipping around the room. Her face seemed familiar to me though and it wouldn't be long before I realised who it was. The bedroom was alive and even my battery pack – Lesley, was awake, which was a first when I was experiencing stuff and I explained to her what was happening and she said,

"You heard what the medium said to you so are you not surprised (very comforting I must say) everyone is trying to reach out to you for messages" I thought about this for a minute and she had hit the nail on the head alright and something needed to be done and quickly. Meanwhile the young girl was still running around the bedroom. Enough was enough and I got out of bed to make a cup of tea for myself and Lesley. As I reached for the tea my eye caught a very old photo of Lesley's sister Christine who had passed away at the very young age of seventeen from a rare blood disorder who I instantly recognised as who was running around our bedroom like a mad thing. I knew I recognised this girl and now it had fallen into place so I tried to link in with Christine and it was fairly easy as she didn't seem to want to go anywhere soon in a hurry. She said and I remember the words so well,

"I haven't spoken to anyone for the last forty odd years and now I can so I will" "Oh great", I thought as dawn was now rapidly approaching and I still had the balcony to deal with. I decided I had to sort out this situation as soon as possible and after a sleepless night and feeling like death warmed up literally and Lesley walking around like a bear with a sore head we both headed for work. I felt dreadful and I suppose Lesley did also for the whole day but somehow we made it through and finally I stumbled through the door feeling worse than ever. I fumbled to find Caroline's number and rang her and she didn't seem surprised either so was this some kind of spirit initiation ceremony I was going through. She explained that spirit would take any opportunity to get a message through knowing that I was a vessel they could channel through and that I should make the rules and tell them when I was ready to receive their messages so I had to be strong and do you know what it worked.

I got into bed and I could feel the faces boring down into mine and I shouted out loud,

"I need my sleep and I make the rules from now on and when I am ready I will let you know when that is but until then I send you my blessings now please return to your realms," which I thought was quite polite as I was so tired. I suddenly began to feel that the faces had greatly reduced in number but some still hung around, so I shouted out suddenly,

"All of you" and then they were gone with the exception of Christine who was quite happy just being there with her sister and myself.

I can't remember falling asleep but I must have done so quite quickly as I slept like a baby that night and Lesley slept well I think as well.

It was the weekend and Christine now wanting to be called Chris was still with me and I began to think that she was part of a bigger picture.

She showed me scenes from her childhood which I would relate too Lesley and the accuracy was amazing down to items in the house they lived in and many times I had Lesley in tears as memories came flooding back and she could once again communicate with her sister that she had been so close to through me.

Chris was going to work with me, and this I had not expected at all, but I was happy to go with it. Chris mentioned a watch she used to have which was still in the family and she wanted me to have it as a memory of her so we went to see Lesley and Chris's Mum to explain about the watch and the strange goings on around me and it was quite moving for her, and she said to me suddenly,

"I know the watch you mean but I have not seen it in the family for years and I think it was lost long ago," Chris was shaking her head in my subconscious and I knew it was in the house somewhere. So where did I go with this now as I had reached a dead end with Lesley's Mum and Chris wasn't having any of it. The conversation changed to other topics less weird and I decided I needed the upstairs toilet so I excused myself and went up and when I had finished and I came back down the passage past Lesley's Mums bedroom I heard a rattling sound and poked my head through the door to see the old fashioned handles swinging on the top drawer of the chest of drawers. I knew this was Chris's work so when I got back downstairs I approached the subject again and got told it wasn't in the house. I said,

"Chris says it's in the top drawer of your chest of drawers" which resulted in quite a heated argument between Lesley her Mum and myself. I think Chris was enjoying this little fracas when Lesley said

"For goodness sake I will look in the damn drawer" and she was up the stairs and pulling the drawer out eventually followed by her Mum and myself. On first inspection there was no watch in the drawer as there were so many trinkets and pieces of bric-a-brac in there. I said, "Chris says its right at the back in a corner" I was as popular as a rattlesnake in a lucky dip at this particular moment as Lesley pulled the whole drawer out with a little more vigour than usual (probably because of Chris and myself) and there in the corner was the watch. Chris had come up trumps this time and a few apologies later with watch in hand we returned home with Chris humming to herself in my head. The watch has stayed on our mantelpiece ever since. Lesley's Mum had offered me the watch by the way, which was a very kind gesture. If I hadn't accepted it I feel my ears would have been ringing for weeks from spirit.

Chris and I were to work together and still do to this day and some of the things she has done have been totally amazing.

Back to the spiritualist church where I was becoming quite well known and on this night we were going to do encaustic art whatever that was but what we did was amazing.

It involved a glossy piece of card, some wax crayons, a cloth and an iron. How strange you may say.

Firstly we did a deep meditation and then you chose the coloured crayons you were drawn to, then colouring in a piece of card with the crayons however you wanted. After that you would cover the card with a cloth and then iron it until the wax melted. The cards were allowed to dry and then members of the circle had to read what they saw in the picture. It was amazing what you could see in these pictures and mine depicted being on a spiritual journey with many ups and downs along the way and I could see where the reader was coming from and everybody else's seemed to be on a similar theme.

We still have the cards at home years later and if you ever get the chance to do one - don't hesitate in my opinion.

A matter of weeks soon went by and I seemed to be developing nicely when Caroline said,

"There is a closed circle Pete that is starting up that I would like you and Lesley to join and I know there are spaces left" and we jumped at the chance but in hindsight it turned out to be a bit of a disaster for me personally.

Caroline bless her, contacted the medium and told her about my potential and that she had already asked us to join. The medium was not happy about this as she had already pencilled in an older couple of her friends since she had last spoken to Caroline but to save embarrassment called her friends and cancelled and very begrudgingly invited us in (you can see where this is going) to her closed circle.

From day one we did not see eye to eye and it was as plain as the nose on your face. The vibes were not good on the first meeting and I felt as if it would only be a matter of time before she found an excuse to get us out and her friends in.

On the first circle night I picked up on energies in the house, which were later validated by Caroline even before the circle had begun for the evening. The accuracy was amazing and involved the medium for the group but she never gave me any encouragement and it felt more like - how could he have mediumship abilities?

It was funny that I never worked well in this circle or even if I did it was never validated and I felt an outcast. Now psychometry has been one of my fortes for many years (the ability to read the energies of an object while holding or touching it) and on this particular night it was on the agenda. I read an object from another person and came up with some rather big revelations, which of course were flatly refuted, and we were marked out of ten at the end and I got a big fat zero.

I thought that was quite good because I expected about a minus sixteen from her and this group, or should I say clique, with the exception of Caroline and Lesley was really getting my goat now. I missed some sessions, as I didn't feel accepted or comfortable in this circle and I was about to pick up the phone to tell the medium that I wasn't coming anymore when Caroline rang to say the medium was ill and she would run the circle from her house that night. It was great as well because Caroline's house was much nearer to ours and there was snow on the roads at the time.

We turned up at Caroline's and as I walked through her door the energies nearly knocked me off my feet as her place was beautiful and I wished we could meet there every week. The circle nearly started late as I was too busy nosing around everywhere studying the objects dotted about and taking in the marvellous energies but Caroline knew me too well and was just happy to see me relaxed and comfortable for once on group night. The circle was opened and I just flew into channelling mode straight away bringing through Caroline's husband who had had his life taken away in a car accident and he had a lovely accurate message for her and Spirit just kept coming and I feel I may have rather hogged the night but this is what I was here to do. It was like I had the shackles removed that usually tied me down on a circle night. At the end of the evening everyone, without exception said how well I had done on the night - especially Caroline. Next week we were back at the mediums house and it couldn't have been more different. She never even said well done to me after everybody had told her how amazing I had been the previous week. It was a clash of personalities with her, and always was, but she also did not like my ghost hunting exploits and she told me so on many occasions. At the end of the session she said,

"Well folks I'm on holiday for the next two weeks (music to my ears) and as Caroline's circle was so good last week I'm happy for it to be carried on there and you never know Pete might come to the party again" and yes she was right. I felt like making the sign of the cross with my fingers in front of her but I kept my cool somehow.

We had two great weeks and I have never felt so confident and happy in a group (until just recently and I still am by the way) giving great messages, good psychometry and trusting in people. Caroline brought out the best in me and could see my potential and I will always be grateful to her.

A fortnight later was to be the last week at the mediums house before the summer break and as usual I was as spiritual and psychic as a brick in her presence and it showed. Once again, she had sucked the spiritual energy out of me and there was no going back. At the end of the session she said,

"I would like you and Lesley to come here at the same time next week so we discuss plans for the next run of closed circles" but I'm psychic as well and call smell a rat from a great distance (did I say I worked in pest control) and this was a rather large one I felt. We both turned up the following week at the agreed time and were greeted with a cup tea and biscuits, which was quite amicable I thought.

She laid it on the line that she did not feel that we were progressing well enough within the group and did not want us in her circle for the next term and felt I was wasting my time trying to be a medium, (you've read my book so far - what do you think) I breathed a sigh of relief inwardly as I could now escape this torture, but my confidence was shattered by her words. I heard after the summer that her two old friends had been brought into the group finally and that things were going really well. Caroline rang us later on that evening to ask us what had been said and when I told her, she was genuinely devastated and did no more than ring the medium and gave her a piece of her mind, which resulted in Caroline walking away from the closed circle and saying to the medium,

"Are you blind? You have just destroyed a good mediums potential" which I thought was rather nice really.

I left the church at this point as I felt I could go no further but it was only the beginning for me, as you will see later but we kept in touch with Caroline though, but very soon she was to move abroad.

Dad's Passing

This was a sad time for all of us, but one of the most amazing also, and I want to share every moment of it with you.

I'm going to start along way back with this and it will all make sense eventually of why I have written it this way.

It was in the army that my Mum and Dad both met and were some of the best times in there lives, (they always show themselves to me in their army uniforms when they come through with messages for family or they need something to be done) and Mum held superior rank to my father which always bugged him. Mum loved it of course and would often wind him up about it but there were never a more devoted couple throughout their lives together. It was wartime in times of the blackouts and such like, and on this particular night they had commandeered an army jeep for the evening. On the way back from an evenings courting, they cut across an airfield in the pitch black when all of a sudden there was a resounding crash and bang as they had driven into a Beau fighter (a WWII fighter plane) and done it a fair bit of damage. I don't really know how they talked their way out of a court marshal but I think Mum had something to do with that in the end. I know its true because I now have the original photographs framed up at home after I managed to find them when we were clearing the bungalow out and I was going to have them and you will see why they became so important to me in the end.

Back to more recent times, as I just wanted to put you all in the picture.

At this time, I was doing quite a fair bit of deep meditation and being given sights of many weird and wonderful things.

Dad was hiding a serious heart condition from us that we did not find out about until after his passing and that's how he wanted it, I think.

He had found it very hard to come to terms with Mum's passing, even though it had been on the cards for a long while and I really feel he just wanted to be with her. A devoted couple for many years and with so many experiences to share regarding bringing up the three of us, like all of us in a Ford Anglia travelling to Sweden which was a major feat and we got there and back safely.

What happened to Scampi was a major upset and with his hidden condition I am surprised that alone didn't take him.

He still had good friends and everybody in the cul-de-sac liked him, especially the old women, who used him as the odd job man even though he was eighty-six years old and with a heart condition. That was my Dad. He would do anything for anybody.

I tried spending as much time with him as I could, especially with him being on his own now. He had a wealth of knowledge and some of our conversations were very long and in depth but we always enjoyed each other's company.

One day, I was at home and during a deep meditation my dear Mum came through still in her army uniform looking very smart as ever. She was stood by the side of an aircraft hanger on an old aerodrome and then she smiled at me with an anxious smile, which wasn't her usual greeting unless something was wrong.

She spoke to me very softy with a tear in her eye and said (I remember these words so well),

"Pete. Tell your father, if he doesn't stop helping people and doing things for others and look after himself, he will be with me sooner than later". That was it and Mum turned, waved and walked away slowly. I love it when Mum comes through but this time I felt it was more than a warning, so I rang my brother and told him what Mum had said to me (Ron, my brother, was a great believer in my abilities and felt we should tell Dad and soon), and he said,

"I am going to see him this afternoon" so we hatched a plan as brothers do. Ron was to go round first and then I would go round later by chance, and start a conversation about my circle and what had happened there with my brother. Dad was very surprised to see me at the door and as he opened it Scampi came running up to me with her ball, the now little spirit dog and Ron shouted,

"Hello little brother what are you doing here"

I replied, "I was just passing and thought I would stop off at the local tea spot" which Mum and Dad's house was famous for, to which many can testify.

Dad said with his unique Irish wit,

"Both of you here together. Has someone died?". How apt, I thought to myself. Dad knew I was attending a Spiritualist Church and was pretty ok with that and what he had seen me do and experience over the years left him in no doubt I was not your average run of the mill son.

I had to give this message to Dad as it was making me uncomfortable and I think that was Mum's doing so we all sat down and before I knew it I was saying out loud,

"Dad, Mum came through with a message for you this morning"

"What did your Mother have to say then" in a thick mellow Belfast accent with a hint of sarcasm,

"She said, if you don't start looking after yourself rather than others you will be joining her sooner than later" which I felt was a better way to put it.

For some strange reason he seemed to accept it without any

"Get out of my house and don't come back" statements,

Had I touched a nerve that I did not know about? After that bombshell, the conversation turned to anything that was not connected to spirit.

Had Dad's inner voice been working on him for a while and this was validation for him, we will never know, but it definitely had an effect and remember, at the time, none of us knew about his heart problems.

Eventually after copious more cups of tea mostly in the

garden as it was such a lovely day, we said our goodbyes and went our separate ways. Back home and chilling out in the evening's fading light I was rudely awakened from my slumber by the phone ringing. I thought it was Ron ringing to say how well Dad had taken the message (how wrong was I) but it was Dad who was more than a little displeased.

He said with no formalities,

"I've been thinking about what you said and your Mother would never have said that and she would never stop me helping people so you're wrong" which was an eye opener to me as any message I get from spirit is usually very accurate.

I replied, "Don't shoot the messenger" and the phone went down and there was no one on the other end but a dialling tone.

I was back in Dad's bad books again which I seemed to have my own chapter in over the years.

Lesley came in from work and I told her what had happened and she said "let the air cool before you contact him again". I felt so guilty but how could I be so wrong and I was still sure I wasn't.

The next day, I heard nothing, and I can't say I wasn't worried at this time but there was a big football match in the evening against local rivals and I was getting ready to go when the phone rang and it was Dad. I tentatively picked up the phone but was surprised when Dad said,

"How are you and are you going to the football tonight"

I said "Yes and I still have a spare ticket if you would like to come with me and I've still got time to pick you up"

He said "That's very kind I would have loved to have come but I have Astronomical Society tonight and I don't want to miss it". This was such a strange conversation to be having with no mention of the previous days events. Other things were said and I write this with a tear in my eye as he said, "I love you son, and we will speak again soon" and the phone went down. This really got to me because he had thrown me a real curve ball that I was just not expecting.

Anyway, I went to the game and we beat our local rivals comfortably and we had retained the local bragging rights for a few more months at least. When I got home I grabbed the phone to ring Dad as I always did if we had won a game but there was no reply so obviously he was still at his Astronomical Society. About eleven forty five that night the phone rang and it was Ron, who said,

"I can't get hold of Dad and I've been trying for ages now"

I said, "Perhaps he's round at a friends having coffee after the meeting" but it was rather late for him to be out and so we left it there until the morning and said "Goodnight".

I had a rather restless night for some reason and we got up fairly early as Lesley had a job interview for a senior position at the local hospital so she was on edge. Just before eight o'clock I tried ringing Dad but again there was still no reply.

Lesley suggested I do a meditation to see if Mum would come through so I went for it and I had been meditating for less than a minute when my Mum appeared and waved at me with a radiant lovely smile on her face still in her army uniform as smartly dressed as ever. She gave no message but as she walked away she was holding the hand of a man in army uniform as they went round the corner. They walked straight past a battered and bruised Beau Fighter and I knew the man was Dad and suddenly they both turned and there were my Mum and Dad standing together waving to me with big smiles on their faces. I was in floods of tears and Lesley knew why. I pulled myself together and said to her,

"Unless this was wrong, Dad had crossed over to the spirit world" and she said,

"I know."

The phone rang suddenly and it was Ron saying "I

can't get hold of Dad still so I going to call round on my way to work in an hour or so,"

I said "You do that but take a key with you so you can get in."

How could I tell him Dad had passed to spirit, he had to find out for himself and I think it was Dad telling me to do it that way.

I waited for the call, which came just a little over an hour later and I held the phone away from my ear and I will never forget Ron's words

"He's dead,"

I can't remember the rest of the phone conversation as it was a blur but very soon we were all at the bungalow with family heading there from all over the country.

Lesley, by the way, had to cancel her interview for obvious reasons but you will be pleased to hear she was given the job at a later date, bless her.

Ron had found Dad in his armchair with a cup of tea still in his hand but it was empty. Dad would not have gone before he'd drank his tea that was for sure. He looked very peaceful and it was later confirmed his heart had just stopped with no pain or trauma, the way I think given the choice, we would all like to go and he deserved that.

Ron and I sat talking to each other on the sofa while dad was in Mum's old armchair which was ironic I felt, and it was as if a surreal sense of calm came over us.

The police and paramedics turned up and did the necessary but one of the policemen had brought his grandma with him (though he didn't realise it) but the message for him was lovely and he went off with an added bonus.

Family arrived from all over and many tears were shed for about half an hour and then the atmosphere seemed to lighten suddenly and on the patio looking in at us sat on a stone bench we had bought Mum and Dad was a beautiful Red Admiral Butterfly - Dad's favourite. We all felt it was a message to say he had crossed over safely and had come back to say goodbye.

Mediums seem to have a way of looking at life and death as a beautiful thing and are able to transmit this to others at the right time and that time was now. Within a very short space of time we were laughing and joking and smiles were back on faces and we knew all Dad wanted was to be back with the love of his life and now he was and in a far better place. Mum's passing seemed to be more of a sombre affair but this was different as it felt like a celebration and I'm sure those in the higher realms were already having a party. When Dad was still in the chair you just knew that his soul had already departed and just the physical body remained.

Dad was born on Friday the thirteenth and his funeral was to take place on Friday the thirteenth, quite ironic really. There were many other connections with Dad and the number thirteen but I can't remember what they were now.

Ron was ferreting about as he usually does and checked dad's phone and the last recorded call was not the one he made to me and no reference to that call was ever found and when I got home and checked my phone there was no record of that call ever having been received. We know he never made it to the Society meeting and he was preparing his dinner, which he would have eaten early, that evening but never got around to it and the rest is a mystery.

The day of his passing was the previous evening but as he was not found until the following day that was when his passing was officially recorded but we know different.

The words "don't shoot the messenger" still ring in my ears to this day and if I ever say it to you just take extra care.

Funeral preparations were coming along well with my help through spirit and hopefully they had everything they wanted on the day.

That day came and it was a typical spring day in May with bluebells just starting to appear en masse in the churchyard, welcoming Dad in as they were his favourite flowers and I couldn't think of a nicer tribute that could be paid to him. As we drove into the car park standing on the left was Dad and I nearly hit him, and without thinking I said "Dads here" all the other occupants in the car looked at me in horror but he had been there and you know what I'm like.

The church was very full and Lesley and myself were sitting in what felt like a fridge for the whole service, as spirit seemed to want to sit with us. There was a lady with a young baby that screamed its head off and had to be taken out when I heard Dad say,

"There's times and places to bring those things and today is not the day". I had a smile to myself and carried on singing to the hymns with a grin on my face and nudging Lesley. Mum had told me what hymns Dad wanted a few days previous and the selection seemed to appeal to everyone. Another job well done I felt.

It was strange to think that I would never be able to ring my parents up on the phone again or could visit the bungalow that had been so full of life until a few days ago, but we had to face the facts that this was now going to be the case. I suppose I should be grateful that I could still communicate with them through the spirit realms.

After the service, which was lovely, and a send off worthy of the great man he was, we headed off for the slow journey to the crematorium.

It was a sad journey and Dad's last of course and many tears were shed along the way. Then it was back to the bungalow for the wake, which was quite a lively affair. I had learnt over recent years that death was not final but just a continuation of the souls journey. Good food, a few drinks and many topics of conversation later it was all over.

Moving on

We were sitting at the table with my uncle Dudley from Belfast and discussing the past and sharing a few memories, as you do on such occasions, when we started to talk about Suffolk and the visits to the Mill and other places in the area when Dudley said,

"It's a shame I never got to see Thorrington Street Mill" and a thought suddenly popped into my head (I do have them occasionally) that as Dudley was staying with us for a few days just perhaps we might be able to take him down there for a day. After speaking with Dudley it was agreed that we would go the following day.

I was excited as I loved Suffolk and the mill and any opportunity to go down there was never ignored as it brought back so many memories.

Auntie Dorry and Uncle Leslie had passed many years ago now but I knew they were buried in Polstead Churchyard, which was quite extensive with many graves and was placed in the middle of the countryside just above the pond that I fished in for so many summers as a boy growing up.

I had a feeling that if the chance arose I would try and find their grave tomorrow on our little outing to Suffolk, but it would be difficult as I didn't know what their grave was like and I knew there were many there. I was sitting quietly before going up to bed, when I got the impression of Auntie Dorry standing in front of me, who I hadn't seen for many years. She smiled and showed me a mental picture of their grave as it was a joint one with a marble headstone but it had a cross on top as well. Before I could blink, she was gone, but it was lovely to have seen her again and I was now determined to find their grave at all costs.

Next morning, I woke early, as it felt like my childhood days going back to Suffolk and still does to this day. Four of us were in the car as we headed east towards Suffolk and the mill.

This was going to be Dudley's day and I had a feeling Mum and Dad had more than a passing interest in it.

The sun was shining on the way down and it was an uneventful journey, but the discussions we had were fun and brought many good memories flooding back. We arrived at the mill in bright sunshine but you must remember the mill was no longer in the family which was a shame as access to the rear of the mill and the pool would possibly not be available now. We arrived with the sun shimmering on the beautiful river Box and rainbow trout were breaking the surface in pursuit of flies, leaving expanding circular ripples on the water. The wind was blowing gently downstream and newly arrived after migrating from Africa the swallows were swooping low over the water in a quest to catch their share of the flies. It was great to be back again after quite a few years but I still had Auntie Dorry's visions bugging me in my head.

There was no one in at the mill, which was a shame, but we did manage to get down along the far side of the riverbank to the mill pool where Mr Scowen had thrown himself in after slitting his throat all those years ago.

Dudley was impressed and wished he had been there when it was still in the Munson family but at least he had seen it now and it always looked an impressive sight whenever we turned up and now was no different.

We left the mill behind and went up to Stoke-by-Nayland churchyard, which was on the way to Polstead, which we would finally reach at some point and if spirit needed me to do something I found myself becoming restless until that mission was completed and this was no different.

In the churchyard were so many Munson graves that it would not be right not to pay our respects. Mum and Dad were also married in the church, which was such a majestic looking building with a big square tower and a quaint little lychgate that they would have walked through on their special day. I wandered off around the back on my own to try and find uncle Joe's grave that wasn't difficult as he was standing by it with that wry smile he always seemed to show. Such a lovely man who was a great part of my childhood and who was also the bailiff for the trout fishing on the river Box and always told me wonderful tales.

He said "Don't forget to visit the 'Queen Mother's' grave if you know what's good for you Pete" that was Joe's name for Auntie Flo. A very large lady with a forthright attitude who had brought Mum up from a child after her parents where both killed in a car accident when she was very young (a very tragic start to her life and considering she lost one of her brothers before he was twenty one as well) and her whole life was changed forever.

I had a few more words with Joe and then he was gone as quickly as he came and I thought I had better go and look then for Flo's resting place but could I find it and it wasn't the smallest plot and ironically I just about tripped over uncle Ron's grave who had been killed in the bicycle accident. We also found Mum's parents grave but sorry Joe the 'Queen Mother' would have to miss out this time.

As I was now freelance ghost hunting I had had some cards made up to pop through doors of places that interested me and one such house across from the church did just that. There was a row of Tudor style buildings (black and white wooden facades) which later turned out to be the old Guildhall, a workhouse and school at one time but not as grand a Guildhall as the inner city ones as we were in the depths of the countryside here. I nipped across the road and after much struggling eventually found a small letterbox and popped a card through but I only found out later that my sister Lynne has a painting hanging in her house of the very same building I was hoping to investigate.

It was now time to head for Polstead and the churchyard and I couldn't wait and as we arrived in the car park it was deserted but a slight drizzle of rain had started.

The type that goes straight through you and soaks you to the skin. Undeterred we started our quest to find the grave of Dorry and Les as it was a combined plot, but there were so many scattered above and below the church it was going to be difficult. The rain was incessant and we were getting soaked but still we continued to search. Where was this grave that I saw from Dorry's vision recently? It couldn't be that hard to find surely, but it was and there was nothing like a marble gravestone with a cross on top anywhere that we could see. I said subconsciously to Dorry,

"Please point us in the right direction to find your final resting place, so we can pay our respects" and it was then the sun peeped through just for a minute and in that time it had lit up a number of gravestones further down the churchyard but none with a cross on top. I went to investigate these few headstones and one had a dark pinkish tinge to it and it was the one that was drawing me. As I approached it from the side I could see it was theirs but where was the cross she had showed me and this puzzled me but I felt that I must read the inscription before I bade them farewell. I stood directly in front of the grave but not standing on it as that would be disrespectful in my opinion so I was further back when I saw it. Just as Dorry had showed me the marble headstone with a cross on top was not visible unless you were standing directly in front of it and the reason being was the grave behind was marked with a stone cross and only from this exact spot could you see a headstone with a cross on it and I was blown away by this. I shouted to the others that I had found it and when they arrived they were amazed. That is why I have put it in the book, as it was such an amazing experience. Thank you Auntie Dorry and Uncle Les for strengthening my belief even further and bless you both.

We left the churchyard and headed on foot down the steep gravel drive through an archway of trees blocking out the natural watery sunshine towards the pond. A couple of young lads were fishing and it brought back instant memories of myself on the same pond all those years ago and with a touch of jealousy I'm afraid. The pond was large and we were all just walking around the far side of it over the very old brick bridge toward Corder's cottage when my phone started to ring with an unknown number. I answered it and was greeted by the voice of the owner of the Tudor style house I had put my card through earlier in the day and he asked if I was still in the area and if so could I call back for a cup of tea and a chat sooner than later. I said it wasn't a problem and all of us agreed as well so we headed back to Stoke-by Nayland and to the house I had been drawn to for some reason. As we pulled up outside the building seemed to take on an even more menacing appearance and I knew my instincts had been right. I knocked the very old iron doorknocker and the sound echoed with an eerie resonance and we could hear footsteps approaching from the other side of the door. The sound of quite a few bolts being drawn back and the creaking of the ancient door as it was opened resulted in quite a young man greeting us. He introduced himself to us and invited us in to the very antiquated building and to our surprise stood up in a corner was a suit of armour and the royal standard of King Richard III. Now this was strange as we lived ten miles from the site of the Battle of Bosworth where Richard was slain and Leicester was where he was supposedly buried (this was long before King Richard's bones were discovered in a Leicester car park by the way) so it took us back a bit. Dudley had stayed in the car, as he wasn't really into all things paranormal and said that he was tired anyway. Back in the house conversation flowed freely and cups of tea and coffee followed on a frequent basis. The young couple had been having many ghostly happenings and regular poltergeist activity (poltergeists are noisy ghosts that like to move objects about and can be pretty frightening to some) and had been trying to get the house investigated for sometime but with no luck so when my card popped through the door it was like a blessed relief to them. I was excited about the possibility of investigating this place and after a guided tour of the house by the couple it was decided that we were more than prepared to run an investigation to find out what was going on there. We had been inside for quite a period of time and longer than we had anticipated but eventually we remerged and as we returned to the car we found Dudley still fast a sleep in the back. A bit strange I thought and I can't say it didn't worry me a little as he wasn't a young man, who used to be very enthusiastic over everything and to see him like this was not the Dudley I remembered. As we waved goodbye to the couple, I shouted out to them that we would be in touch very soon, but I still hated leaving this part of the world even now as it brought back so many childhood memories for me but to think I would be back soon lessened the blow. Dudley had been staying with us over the period of the funeral, as we would never have let him stay in a hotel after all he had done for us over the years. It had been nice to show him around where we lived and somewhere he had always wanted to see but the following day he was to leave and it would be the last time we would see him. We arrived back home safely in the late evening after a very tiring but eventful and enjoyable day in Suffolk and my thoughts immediately changed to the planning of the up and coming ghost hunt. We took Dudley to Narborough station the next day and as he climbed aboard and shut the carriage door of the train I felt a tinge of sadness and strangely enough a tear appeared in my eye as he disappeared into the distance for what was to be the last time though I did not know it.

As things started to return to normal or as best they could we had to think about putting parent's bungalow up for sale, which was going to be a difficult time for all of us. There was so much stuff to go through in the house, and many of the items would carry specific memories, so tears and laughter would never be far away while this process was being carried out.

Unbeknowing to me, earlier in the year, my sister and

husband had arranged to take Dad to France and Belgium for the sixty fifth anniversary of Dunkirk as he had been one of the last to be evacuated from the beach at Bray Dunes during World War II, but to my surprise Lesley and myself were invited to take his place and we both eagerly agreed when offered. Perhaps my sister had made a pact with spirit but I really wasn't prepared for the events that were about to take place.

It was a busy Friday before the Whitsun Bank Holiday as we slowly crawled our way through the near stable traffic and over the Dartford Bridge towards Dover and the trailer tent waiting for us situated a few miles from the ferry terminal to Calais.

The campsite was quite nice and after a hot cup of tea we all decided to settle down and make plans for the following day but nothing was going to go to plan as Dad would see to that. It was then the first train went by and trying to hear ourselves speak was a major undertaking so we decided to reconvene at a local pub where we could have a nice hot meal and discussion in a more relaxed atmosphere. I could not help but think that the trains would make sleep nigh on impossible where the trailer tent was situated.

The ferry was booked for six o'clock the next morning so we were up before five and soon down at the ferry looking out over a rather calm sea and wondering what the day would bring. I can't say any of us weren't tired after the relentless sound of trains through the night and the early start but this day was in memory of dad so it was best foot forward. The ferry journey was calm and uneventful which was very pleasing as I could be sick on a barge, trust me! Soon we had our land legs again and were in the car heading for Calais and City Europe, which was a massive shopping centre. While walking around I nipped to the toilet and as I came out I noticed a mural on the opposite wall which depicted, to my surprise, the beach and cliffs at Cuckmere Haven where my parents ashes were to be scattered in the not to distant future. Suddenly I began to see the image of a large tank heading towards me along the corridor and I knew Dad had joined us. Once outside everything seemed to have changed and I could hardly breathe due to smoke and the noise of a dog fight being carried out in the skies above me. I relayed this to the others and none of them seemed to bat an eyelid at what I was telling them, it was as if they were expecting it. The cacophony of noise at times was unbearable, and I felt more than a little uncomfortable in my current surroundings with blimps dotted around the skyline and ak-ak fire following the searchlights. I was glad to get into the car and head for somewhere more peaceful because the scenes I was experiencing were more than a little disturbing right then. I felt Dad's energy sitting next to me in the car and I knew he wanted me to experience some of what he had gone through as he had never really talked about it while he was alive.

All of a sudden the visions stopped and I had time to catch my breath and regroup my thoughts after an eventful start to proceedings. We were now driving down long straight roads with fields as far as the eye could see on either side with memorials dotted here and there in memory of soldiers who gave their lives in both World Wars. Soon we were approaching a more built up area which turned out to be the outskirts of Veurne in Belgium. A beautiful little town reminiscent of Austria in my opinion. As we drove along, Dad whispered,

"That is the church where we had to take shelter during a shoot out in amongst the grave stones," so we stopped and had a look around and the energies were strong in that place. Once back in the car, we headed into Veurne for a coffee and a bite to eat in the town square which was bustling with folk while in the background the church clock chimed while a much deeper bell sound resonated from the Town Hall. It was a place I could have spent the whole day in, willingly, but as it was only a day visit we soon had to move on. Back in the car again, which was a good job as the heaviest rain I had seen in a long time battered the roof of the car and the streets were a wash with dirty turbulent water cascading here, there and everywhere. It was over in minutes and we were left wondering what had just happened. We now headed towards Ypres in Belgium where Dad had spent some time during the conflict but doing what, we didn't know. We pulled up along side a large wide river while my sister Lynne passed around the sandwiches and bits she had painstakingly prepared the previous day. As I got out of the car I could hear shouting and began to see troops in khaki fatigues putting pontoons together across the river which was quite an undertaking as the water was turbulent and pushing through, totally different to how I was seeing it today as I stood there realising that this was what dad had been involved in. Now, with bellies full, we headed for further adventures on this quickly changing day in the direction of Bray-Dunes when Dad said,

"Watch out for the unusual windmill up the road, you can't miss it,"

There was no windmill we could see until finally we turned into a small village and there on the other side was a windmill I have never seen the like of before. It was made from wooden slats and was quite an imposing feature on the bleak landscape and I gathered that this was the one he meant but time was not on our side so I thanked him and we carried on. We soon passed another church where Dad wanted us to stop as some of his comrades were laid to rest there so out of respect we did that for him and shared a prayer out of respect. It was a very moving period of time we spent observing the rows of graves and memorials to the dead of both wars. Feeling very sombre, now we drove towards the coast when Dad showed me the picture of a building with a bright red tiled roof out in the countryside. Now remember, we were in a strange country we knew very little about, but trusting in my Dad was now becoming part of the itinerary on this little jaunt. We travelled for a while with Dad pointing various things out which I had got used to by now (don't you just love spirit?) but this red roofed building had been eluding us as we drove into the town of De Panne when Dad suddenly shouted in my ear,

"Turn right here, It's down here, I remember now", so one sharp turn later and we were heading down a rather bumpy, dusty lane with what looked remarkably like a red roofed building in the distance. As we pulled up we could all see it was an old railway station with a red tiled roof like I had been shown but was now in disrepair and needed more than a bit of tender loving care. Dad said,

" This was a very poignant place as the troops had held up here one night for safety while gunfire, bombs and general mayhem continued all round as they waited to make the push towards Bray-Dunes and the thought of freedom from this hell hole." He began to show me scenes of death and destruction and I could taste and smell the oil and fumes in my nostrils and on my lips when suddenly he said,

"I don't want to show you anymore of this as you wouldn't sleep at night. Very thoughtful, I thought to myself, but I could understand where he was coming from and was quite grateful when the scene reverted to modern day. We left the area and headed towards our final destination on this quest to visit Bray-Dunes which had been Dad's intention all along and soon we could see the sea in the distance.

We parked the car and climbed up the concrete steps to the palisade above the beach and looked onto the sands that had seen so much action during the war, which is now known, as the Dunkirk evacuations. There was a memorial to the brave soldiers who lost their lives on that beach and sixty five years on I felt quite privileged to be standing there, honouring the fallen and the many troops who survived and made it back to England safely on the many ships that braved the bombardments brought upon them by the Germans. Dad didn't show me anything that went on at the beach as I feel I had been shown enough and we now appreciated what he and his fellow comrades went through. Dad made it off the beach in a small coal boat and I will be forever grateful for the captain and crew that saved him in the last few hours before the evacuation effort was called off or I wouldn't be here writing this book now.

The rest of the day visit went off without incident and eventually we found our way back to Calais and the waiting ferry to take us back to Dover. One thing I noticed as we boarded the ferry was the flags nearly being ripped of their poles and large waves lashing against the side of the boat as a storm had developed during the day which would make the journey across the channel more than uncomfortable for us and with my track record I was more than a bit worried and I will leave it at that! One other thing that happened on the way back was Dad popping up at one point and saying,

"Once I saw the white cliffs of Dover I knew I was home safely and I shed a tear and thanked God."

I hope he enjoyed his trip with us back to Dunkirk and we all certainly learnt much that day thanks to him.

Bless you Dad.

The Ashes Saga

We were all at the bungalow one afternoon sorting out boxes of books as both parents had been avid readers in their time when Lynne asked where Scampi's ashes where as they had never been scattered and Dad had passed quite quickly following the incident with the little dog which was so traumatic for him. Well we searched the bungalow high and low but they were nowhere to be found and we didn't even know how they had been preserved which didn't help matters. When Mum had passed we had a tree planted in her name in the local arboretum which showed her name, dates and the words,

"Light's out" to remind her of her war years which she talked so fondly about as it was when she met my father. This was written on a brass plaque on a post. Since Dad's passing we had had another plaque made up with the words,

" The perfect gentleman with his feet on the ground and his head in the stars," and fitting for a man with such a wealth of knowledge of the universe. We had thought that perhaps Scampi's ashes should be scattered there as it was now our family's focal point and as there were no graves to visit due to parents being cremated, but we had to find them first and foremost.

We all sat down for lunch and a well-earned rest but still the mystery of Scampi's ashes loomed large so I quietly asked spirit if they would help us locate them.

All of a sudden from the hallway came a bang and a scraping noise, which seemed funny as all the doors were locked so no one could come in without ringing the doorbell for us to answer first so we all got up at once to see what it was and the strangest thing had happened. The glass cabinet with all their precious ornaments in had one of it's doors wide open and a space where a Waterford Crystal elephant had stood for many a long year. I had been promised I would be left this along with the

Waterford Crystal lamp by Mum so I knew she was about and trying to help. Where could it have possibly gone I wondered and now we had two objects missing or had apported for some reason (an apport is when spirit moves an object from one place to another) so the plot thickened? Hours more went by in this elephant and ashes hunt, but nothing had turned up, so where else could we look? It really only left the garage, which was large and quite high with two levels of shelving all the way round. Well if you thought the house was cluttered you needed to take a look in the garage as it was worse and a real Aladdin's Cave. I could not begin to mention the plethora of objects that we found in this place but at one point Ron and I noticed at the same time the crystal elephant hanging precariously off one of the shelves but it was too high for us to reach without ladders so while one of us went to fetch some step ladders from the kitchen, the other stayed and made sure it didn't fall or try and disappear by itself again. Ron arrived back with the ladders and he climbed up and safely brought down the elephant without breaking it but as he did so he noticed a brown box behind it. Out of curiosity he grabbed the box also and brought that down and on it were the words Scampi's Ashes, we had found them with the aid of a little help from the other side.

That weekend was lovely and warm and with the smell and the colours of the meadow flowers enveloping us we scattered Scampi's ashes around the base of the tree and we all said a little prayer, thanked our parents and made our way back to the bungalow for coffee.

It is amazing what spirit are capable of and over the years I have learned to trust in them.

The Waterford lamp and crystal elephant now take pride of place in our house and are always on display. As a reminder of my parents and what they are still capable of from the spirit side of life.

We still had my parent's ashes to scatter but there would be a time and a place for that before too long which would turn out to be a memorable occasion also.

Onwards and Upwards

It was a few days later that Caroline Clare rang one evening to say that she needed to see us as she had some news, but what could that be we wondered to ourselves. We arranged to pay her a visit the next evening to find out. So the next evening we knocked the door and ventured into her house which always mesmerised me with all it's artefacts scattered about. The smell of incense filled the air and tickled my nostril hair making me sneeze which over powered the aroma of fresh ground coffee being brewed in the kitchen. Egyptian pictures hung from the walls along with portraits of Elvis as Caroline was a big fan still and she even had a model of Graceland on the sideboard. She was always the most gracious of hosts, and you felt like you didn't want to leave at the end of the evening. Before I knew it, Caroline had thrown me a ring to practice my psychometry on and as usual I came up with the goods within a few minutes that pleased her. Then she dropped a real bombshell when she said, "Sorry folks but I'm moving to France as I need a new start and an opportunity has arisen I just can't ignore," and we were both taken aback to say the least and it took a while to sink in. My mentor and guide, through everything spiritual, was moving away so now whom could I turn to?

She continued, "I have taught you much and you must continue on this path and doors will open for you along the way when you least expect it but keep going as you are going to make a very good medium one day". These words filled me with great happiness and gave me great belief in my abilities but I still needed to trust. Then she went on to tell me how to find my spirit guides as they would have great wisdom and would help me along the path I was travelling and then she said,

"Have you heard of the lift method?"

"What's that?" I said, and she began to explain. It involves two lifts during meditation, one you are travelling in upwards and the other will come towards you from the spirit realms and the object is for both lifts to end up side by side with their doors open and that is when you will be introduced to your spirit guide. Sounds fun I thought so I gave it a try but got absolutely nowhere. Caroline laughed and said,

"It's not that easy Pete, but keep trying and if you trust in spirit it will happen eventually for sure". That's what I liked about Caroline, she would do anything to help anyone and always made you feel comfortable with anything you tried.

She had sold her lovely house and it was doubtful we would see her again so at the end of the evening we all felt a little sad and her last words to me before we left were,

"Make me proud, I am trusting in you,." Wow those words were powerful and I wondered what would be coming next as Caroline had always been right in the past and would I ever see her again and a tear began to well in my eye's.

I had not been near a spiritualist church since I had knocked the stuffing out of me a while ago now but I suddenly and for no apparent reason had the urge to go back, probably because I had lost my mentor and rock in the shape of Caroline Clare.

I knew there was another one in Leicester but where it was I had no idea, but it was soon to fall into my lap quite by chance.

When we got back from Caroline's, still trying to take in her news I noticed there was an answer phone message that had been left so I went to check it. It was from a work colleague's wife who knew that I could channel spirit and she had a friend who was having trouble with an angry ghost in her house or so she thought. I rang her back and said I could help if she could arrange the details and that was all I needed to know and then I noticed another message and this was from the couple at Stoke by Nayland offering us a date for an investigation at their house. Two significant messages within a few minutes from arriving back from Caroline's, boy was she good I thought to myself. When I got to work the next day my colleague told me his wife had arranged for us to visit her friends on Friday evening and we were to meet them there.

Lesley and myself arrived there just after seven o'clock in the evening and our friends were already parked up. We knocked on the door and a fairly young chap and his wife opened the door and as they did so you could cut the air with a knife, such negativity and I could tell there was some rift in this relationship. After we were all introduced, sat down and offered a hot drink I asked if there was any friction between the couple and the husband immediately denied it but I knew different. His wife was in the kitchen banging about as she could clearly hear the conversation going on and I bet if I had asked her first she would have said yes. As we sat in the strange atmosphere a wedding photo visibly threw itself off the wall and the glass smashed on the floor and we all looked at each other in disbelief but the wife said,

"Now do you think we have a problem?"

"Yes I do" I replied quite taken aback, then all of a sudden I began to build up a picture of a small man in a cap carrying a walking stick and walking through fields of sheep. The roads around him were like gravel tracks which wound up and down steep hills and when I relayed this to the wife, she asked me if could I tell her where in the country this would be. In the background I could see a river and above it a large mansion house which I recognised to be in Derbyshire and with that she smiled and said,

"That's my granddad, he worked on the estate as a gamekeeper many years ago". Brilliant I thought, but now I had to find what he wanted and it wasn't difficult to work out that he was frustrated by the arguments that were going on the house and he was trying to protect his granddaughter but how could I say this to them in the most politically correct way possible without causing offence. This was going to be a test of development so I said,

" Your Granddad says there is friction between both of you at the moment and it is unnecessary and it needs to stop" but again the husband denied this, so I replied with my favourite response,

"Don't shoot the messenger," and left it like that. Meanwhile, his wife called me into the other room and showed me a photo of her Granddad at work and to my surprise it was exactly as he had shown himself to me earlier. Then she said quietly,

" You are exactly right you know with what you are saying, and we are going through a difficult period right now and as soon as you leave he will be at it again, shouting and throwing things about",

" I said Granddad won't stop you know, until you do something about it."

I heard from my colleague a short while later that they had gone their separate ways and I breathed a sigh of relief. While I was chatting with him I asked if he and his wife would be interested in a stay at the Inn on the Moor and guess what he said,

" Yes", and I could now feel it pulling me back but we had another investigation before that in Suffolk.

I rounded up a small bunch of us including Ron, Christine and Lesley and armed to the teeth with paranormal ghost hunting equipment we headed for the old guildhall.

It was a Friday afternoon when we left as we had all agreed to finish work early that day to allow time for the five-hour drive. It was raining heavily as we left and wasn't until we were beyond Cambridge that the sun peeked its head out from behind the clouds for a few minutes but long enough to see a double rainbow, something I had never seen before. Could this be an omen I thought to myself, and hopefully a good one when it came to it. We made far better time to our destination than first planned so when we arrived our hosts were not back yet and as there was a nice public house round the corner we all took a gentle stroll to get something to eat in the summer sunshine. Our hosts eventually came and joined us and a lovely evening was had by all, but things would change rapidly back at their house. As we left the pub the sky looked angry and fork lightning raked across the sky lighting up the whole village and followed by loud bellowing thunder, which added to the ambience I felt. The rain started to come down in torrents and the road was now a river, as the water was sucked down the drains and making a gurgling sound as it went but as soon as it started it seemed to have stopped and only the distant rumble of thunder remained, a bit of a pity really. As our hosts opened the front door with its tell tale creak we went straight inside and before we get our coats off a large ripping sound and crash came from the hallway. When we went to investigate we found the big wooden coat rack in the middle of the floor but broken as well. That was a welcome we thought. A warm cup of coffee was the order of the day but you had to be careful where you sat as there was a whole litter of kittens wreaking havoc and I could see one hanging off King Richard III's replica suit of armour which puts you in the picture. Finally they seemed to settle down and normal service was resumed and our hosts updated us on what had happened since we last were there and it seemed quite a bit had. While we were all talking I noticed a figure forming in front of the fireplace and he looked of medium build with a black cloak and a black top hat and I was not the only one seeing this as now all the cats and kittens were staring in the same direction which was quite spooky in itself, I felt. Suddenly he started to move and I could see him climbing the stairs so I grabbed a camera and with Ron following we headed after him as I thought he had gone into one of the bedrooms. Others in the group were off taking photos and trying to capture voice recordings in various areas while Ron took a photo in one of the bedrooms and caught an orb on the wall. I challenged this entity and each photo taken showed the orb getting larger and larger until it really was the size of a beach ball. I was given the impression that he had been a pretty evil man in his day and that he had been in charge of the orphanage and workhouse but he had also done some despicable deeds in his time and his energy was negative. He didn't like what I was accusing him of and suddenly he left the room and next thing a table lamp went flying down the stairs followed by a bright red ball which bounced its way down without any human help, and then he was gone. The atmosphere seemed to lift all of a sudden and you could feel the house warming up and then silence with the exception of occasional camera clicks. Our hosts had invited us to stay the night as it was too far to travel back home without any sleep so we all snuggled down where we could and nothing else happened, it was like a different house. In the morning after copious cups of coffee we said our goodbyes and left. No further activity had been recorded during the remainder of the night so possibly by outing the secrets of this entity I had finally driven him from his refuge. The couple thanked us again and said they would contact us if they had any further issues but to date I have heard nothing.

Now that investigation was finally put to bed, my thoughts turned to the Inn on the Moor once again and when our friends would want to go and hopefully it wouldn't be too long. Back at work, I caught up with my colleague and between us we agreed on the spring bank holiday as the time for our visit to the Inn so I rang up that night thinking any chance of the two usual rooms had long since gone but to my surprise they were the only two vacant on both the Friday and Saturday nights and it was as if it was meant to be. Obviously I booked them there and then while they were still available as I could not believe my luck and our friends were delighted when I rang them and told them the news, but would they be so delighted after the stay I wondered.

It was forecast to be a really hot holiday weekend so we took the sports convertible and headed to Cornwall with the wind blowing in our faces all the way and it was exhilarating to say the least. It was really hot as we turned down the lane towards the Inn and I began to feel the usual presence of the children who must have enjoyed riding in a sports car. Our friends had not arrived yet so we decided to go and get a drink before booking into our rooms for the two nights and it wasn't long before they arrived and did the same. There was a lovely cooling breeze blowing through the courtyard as we sipped our drinks in the baking sun and wondering what lay before us in the nights ahead at this place. Once we had finished our drinks we all fetched our bags from the cars and headed for reception were we were given our keys before we made our way up the stairs and along the uneven corridor to the dark and gloomy far end. One thing though, it was nice and cool up here as our friends turned the key in the lock to their room only to be greeted as they opened the door by a small stool crashing into the door and a shadow figure disappearing into the en suite bathroom followed by an ear piercing scream from my friends wife who was now petrified and seriously considering returning home to safety. That must have been a record for activity in that place as it started so quickly and it was a good twenty minutes before we had calmed his wife down. Finally we were getting somewhere and things had settled back down and we hadn't even opened our own door yet which I was really looking forward to. It was soon our turn and as I opened the door I can't say I was more than a little disappointed when nothing happened but that's ghost hunting for you. We had a rest for an hour or so before going to dinner and I soon dozed off and yes I actually did get some sleep as the drive had taken its toll. I was woken by Lesley who was rummaging about in our bags trying to find something to wear for dinner and I was feeling really hungry now and the smells from downstairs weren't helping matters either. We knocked on our friend's door but they weren't quite ready so we went in and waited when suddenly I began to feel really nauseous and my stomach was off for some reason and I had no idea why but any thought of eating food was gone from my mind very quickly. Had I been hit by the energy of a spirit or something that had tried to take me over I wasn't sure as I had to watch the others eat but it really didn't bother me now. They all enjoyed their meals, lucky them, and on the way back to our rooms we detoured by the gift shop, which was full of goodies and I was looking for one particular item and that was the pen with the coloured lights in the top which span around and the spirit children loved. I eventually found them and there were only two left so we bought both so our friends could have one as well. We headed back to our rooms for a few minutes as I was still feeling pretty rough but all of a sudden it just lifted like it had never been there in the first place and I must put it down to the paranormal. I pressed the light pen and it lit up our whole room and then left it on our bed while our friends did the same with theirs but left it on the dressing table in front of a large mirror. We decided to go and have a drink downstairs in the bar as I now felt I was back to normal once again but it was hunger that was the issue now and after a pint of cider and a couple of packets of cheese and onion crisps I felt a little less hungry but it was no substitute for a good hearty meal I'm afraid. The same proprietor as before recognised me and came across to see if we wanted to do another investigation because if we did he would leave everywhere unlocked for a couple of hours so we gratefully accepted his offer. This being the case, we ventured back to our rooms to pick up cameras and voice recorders when our friends noticed they could not find their light pen and they searched high and low but could not find it anywhere. Ours was still on our bed where we had left it but then we noticed another one precariously balanced on the trouser press in the corner of our room and nobody had put it there that was for sure. Both rooms had been locked when we went for a drink so the pen must have apported from one room to the other. That shocked our friends and with that we made our way back downstairs to start our investigation in the lounge area that was now closed off for the night but only a few orbs were caught in this area so we moved on to the smuggler's museum. All the exhibits and lights had been switched off for the night and torches and night vision cameras were all we had as we groped our way around, when all of a sudden one of the animated exhibits at the other end of the museum started working for no apparent reason which made us all jump and this was followed by a smell of what could only be described as resembling rotten eggs. That smell is supposed to denote a negative spirit present, but I think someone had eaten too much or was it just jealousy on my part. Nothing else of any note happened downstairs so we locked up after us and gave the keys back. The proprietor asked if we had experienced anything and we told him about both the incidents in the smuggler's museum which seemed to interest him and he told us the exhibits were on a timer and would not come back on again until the morning. This had been experienced before along with the reports of a bad smell. We all headed back up the stairs and along the uneven corridor which had begun to take on a sinister appearance as the light was fading fast and the ghouls were hopefully coming out to play now. My mission was to get to the biscuits with the complimentary tea and coffee as they were a food source and I was hungry right now. Biscuits devoured and a nice cup of coffee later, we were all ready to go again and we decided to start in our room this time so lights off and cameras on and we experienced nothing but a few orbs in the space of forty five minutes, how disappointing we all thought. After another cup of coffee to keep us awake we moved to our friend's room, which, by the way, had loads of chocolates and other goodies to help my hunger pangs, which was great. We settled down and off went the lights and despite asking out very little was happening until we heard three rhythmic taps that came from the wall and we all got excited but they were never repeated again. The girls decided to go outside for a cigarette leaving my work colleague and myself alone in the room with whatever it could throw at us. I was looking through the view finder of the night vision camera when from the door came what I can only describe as a bright white dancing snake like thing which moved around the room in no particular direction. As is nearly always the case, I did not have my camera running, which really infuriated me. I decided to leave it running this time and managed to catch a necklace of orbs dripping out of the dressing table mirror but when I played it back you could only just make the orbs out very faintly. The girls had not yet returned when a number of bright orbs shot across the room and were clearly visible with the naked eye and what interested us were the variety of colours amongst them. When the girls returned the activity seemed to cease so after a few minutes they went to make a coffee as it was now the early hours of the morning and they were feeling tired probably from the lack of activity. Once again these bright coloured orbs reappeared but fewer in numbers this time and it was more than obvious that they were afraid of the girls for some reason, but we never found out why. It had been a slow night really, but that's what you can get when you are hunting ghosts, so no footsteps along the corridors or bangs or bumps this time, only the strange happenings that I have already discussed that we had experienced earlier. Breakfast was a real treat in the morning and I think I rather pigged out but who could blame me as I was so hungry. The next day was rather warm and we headed to the seaside but everybody seemed to have the same idea I think and the roads were choked up with traffic and parking anywhere was becoming a nightmare. So after a pretty stressful day, we returned to the Inn and we all had a good meal that evening with no repeats of the previous night thank goodness. After a few drinks we decided to let nature take its course and if anything happened, it happened, and if not, so be it. We were all tired and ready for a good nights sleep. Nothing of any consequence happened in either room over night, and I slept fairly well for a change. A massive breakfast greeted us in the morning and it was just what we all needed before the long journey home. We said our farewells to the proprietor and thanked him for allowing us once again into places we would not normally be able to get to and promised him once again that anything we captured he could have a copy of but we really didn't catch anything.

Back at home it was time to get ready for work after a fun filled long weekend and I was working in Leicester city centre. I had a new client I had to visit and when I had finished, I cut up some side streets to save a bit of time when I passed a large building on a corner with big brown front doors and large panes of glass so you could see inside. It looked a little like a church foyer until I started to read the posters which were advertising medium development and various work groups and I realized this was the other spiritualist church that I had stumbled across by chance. I tried the door and it was locked much to my bitter disappointment but for some reason this place felt right to me and I had to investigate it further of that there was no doubt.

It would be three or four weeks later that I would finally satisfy my curiosity and find out what lay beyond the doors of Leicester Progressive Spiritualist Church and it would be worth the wait. I was busy with my job and as I worked in other areas besides Leicester it had to be put on the back burner for now, but very soon I was to be distracted anyway, as on a sunny day while driving through Derbyshire, I received a phone call that would rock me to the core. It was from my Aunt in Belfast with some terrible news that Dudley had passed to spirit. I pulled into the nearest layby to collect my thoughts. Earlier that day I had been working in the cellar of a public house when the lights had started to flicker and strange noises were happening all around that I could not explain and I had thought to myself spirit are trying to get my attention but I shut them out by saying,

" I'm trying to work here and how would you like it if you were in my position right now, so please let me get on with my job and come through at the appropriate time, thank you", I can't say I didn't feel a little bit guilty right now as it was probably Dudley who was trying to communicate with me all along. He was found in bed curled up in a foetal position and his heart had stopped just like Dad's had, which I found quite ironic. Now Dad and Dudley had crossed over in the space of a few short months and by the end of that year a total of six close relatives would have left us forever, including Aunt Pansy who made her journey on New Years Eve. I would not be able to attend his funeral as I had just started my new job and I did not have sufficient holidays available to me, at this time but Ron and Christine possibly could if they cut their holiday short on the Isle of Man. Once I had managed to get hold of them to relay the bad news, they seemed intent on getting to his funeral even if it was in Belfast, but after making plans and booking their hotel for the night everything seemed to conspire against them to stop them getting there. The night they had booked to stay in the hotel a major riot broke out around that area. A ton of damage was done and some people were injured so was this Dudley protecting Ron and Christine we will never know, but once again, I have my suspicions.

Finally, I was back working in the city centre once again and I had planned my day so my lunch break could be taken if I gained access to the church at that time. About twelve thirty I arrived on the stone steps and I pushed the front door but once again it was locked much to my dismay. I was about to leave when I noticed a doorbell on my left. There were no lights on that I could see but I rang it anyway but nothing happened, so with a heavy heart I turned to leave when suddenly a light turned on in the foyer and shortly after a middle aged man turned the key in the lock and opened the once impenetrable door and let me in. After introductions he offered me a cup of tea and I duly obliged knowing I could spend the best part of an hour here and I felt in no hurry to leave. Inside was much larger than the first impressions I had originally made of the place when failing to gain access. I followed this chap upstairs, not knowing what to expect but I felt more than comfortable and an air of peace and calm seemed to envelop me. Upstairs was a small church with a rostrum and rows of seating and a kitchen at the rear and there were posters everywhere advertising various events and workshops open to everyone, even me. He asked me why I had come today and soon we were in a very long drawn out conversation and he could see by my enthusiasm that I felt right at home there. I told him of many of my experiences and readings that I had done, which he seemed very interested in but time was not on my side as my lunch break was nearly over before it had started. I was so lost in conversation that I hadn't noticed the time and he suggested I come back again and meet Marian whom he thought would be very interested in my story as hopefully you are, reading this. On the way downstairs he opened the door on the left into the large church where I was completely blown away by the majesty of the place and I thought to myself I wonder how many mediums had taken to that stage over the years and brought validation and closure to so many and I was now in my element and I knew it.

I couldn't wait to tell Lesley about this church when I got home and the good feelings I had about it which would only intensify over time and springboard me into the world of mediumship.

Learning from Spirit

It was a hot summers day and the skylarks were chattering high above the golden ripe cornfields and combine harvesters could be heard bailing the hay in the distance. Kids were rolling down the hills of the luscious green meadows and laughing and joking as they were on holiday and without a care in the world much like myself. Samba my black Labrador was playing hide and seek in amongst the corn and raising every partridge he could find as was his nature being a gun dog. I was in a really peaceful place right now when thoughts of the 'lift method' and Caroline suddenly came to mind for no apparent reason but it wouldn't hurt to give it a try anyway. I tried to clear my mind of everyday rubbish and asked spirit to help me find my spirit guide as I started to imagine myself inside a lift travelling upwards with the doors tightly closed, while another was travelling from the spirit realms towards me. I had tried this on numerous occasions but for some reason I had got absolutely nowhere, but today somehow it felt right and very soon my lift stopped with a bump and I also felt the other lift from spirit do the same. I waited for sometime and then my door started to open at the same time as the other lift door opened and I walked slowly through, with some trepidation I might add. Before I knew it, I was grabbed on either arm by two Indian braves who unceremoniously dragged me out of the lift and up many stone carved steps on the side of a mountain and onto a plateau. I was stood in front of a circle of stones with a large crackling fire in the middle with smoke spiralling up from it forming different animal shapes which I found rather unusual. Around it were a group of native Indians beautifully dressed and sat cross legged looking at me and some of the faces seemed a little familiar. As I looked further round I was greeted by the smile of a large Native American Indian who beckoned me forward with a reassuring manner. He had a weather beaten face and was covered in strings of beads of unimaginable colours and spoke in a very calming voice, not what I had expected from this big man of whom I was in total awe at this precise moment when suddenly he spoke,

"Peter, it is a long time since we last met but the time is now right",

I said, "We have met before then?"

His reply, "Many times, my friend and you have much to learn once again. My name is Dancing Cloud and I have guided you many times before, and do so again now". Wow! I thought to myself, this is amazing,

He continued, "Come sit with me and we shall journey now together" - whatever that meant. I sat down on mats of once again incredible colours that were beyond description and I was passed a peace type pipe. He smiled and motioned me to draw on it and within seconds I was flying high above the plateau and surveying all below through the eyes of an eagle then swooping down over the rivers and the heavily clad pine forests with the smell invigorating my nostrils. I glided on the thermals, then high over villages and towns before returning back to the plateau and my most gracious host.

He said " The eyes of the eagle will guide you through life when you want to see all that is before you from a distance, so you can take everything in". I thanked him and he continued,

"That is all for now, but visit again soon so I can continue your training or if you need to know anything", and with a wave of his large hand he was gone and I was back on the old disused railway path as if nothing had happened, but it had. I wasn't expecting that I thought to myself with a spring in my step as we continued our walk and I looked forward to the next time I would meet with Dancing Cloud. As I was walking I thought he did say if I had any questions to ask, so subconsciously I asked, if you are my guide can you give me some concrete proof (a little pushy I know) but I had to be sure I wasn't hallucinating in any way. Within seconds I was shown a picture which looked like seven Native Indians standing in a row but it was in a large book and the picture was on the right hand page near the bottom - but why I wondered, and it wasn't until I was back home that I found out. Arriving back, I unclipped Samba's lead and clicked the kettle on for a well earned cup of coffee still with thoughts in my head of what had just happened. I settled down and began to think where I could find information on Native American Indians and where to find this picture of validation which I knew was for me to find. The Internet was too vast, it would be like looking for a needle in a haystack though, so I went on a book hunt as I had been shown the picture that way. After a fruitless hour or so, I gave up a little more than frustrated. There just were no books in the house on Native Indians - or so I thought - until I went into the sun lounge for another cup of coffee and as I was sitting my eyes were being drawn to a handful of books in a small bookcase and one in particular which was about our history through the years. I grabbed it and noticed one of the pictures on the front showed a Native American Indian and my heart leapt a little bit. I opened up the index and looked for Native American Indians and there were about a dozen pages on the subject, so I turned to them but no picture could I find that resembled the one that I had been shown. I felt gutted and proceeded to put the book back in the case and finish my now cold cup of coffee but I was still getting the familiar hair tickling which meant to me that spirit are agitated for some reason. Then I heard in my ear the words Alaskan and Canadian which was rather strange but I went with it and fetched the book once more from its shelf. I again went to the index and looked up Alaskan and Canadian Native Indians and to my surprise there was a section exactly entitled that, so I turned to it. Nothing on the first page, but as I turned it over I nearly dropped the book as there was the very same picture in exactly the same position as I had been shown during the very eventful dog walk earlier in the day. It turned out that the seven Native Indians were standing in a large dug out canoe and were hunters and fur trappers. There was a good written piece about these Natives and how they lived and as I read on, it became more and more interesting. For instance, they were known as the most spiritual of all tribes and they worshipped the orca (killer whale), butterfly, eagle and the wolf which happened to be the first four tattoos I ever had. They were very much into tattooing in their own unique style though, so was this a coincidence, I don't think so and as far as I'm concerned there is no such thing as coincidence only spiritual manipulation. You must have thought to yourselves at one time or another that a certain coincidence was beyond the realms of possibility and you were right – I believe it wasn't. What spirit is capable of, we really cannot comprehend but I just go with it now and enjoy the experience knowing that they are around me.

After this revelation, I decided I must go back to speak with Dancing Cloud to find out more so I did no more than put on my Native American flute music (funny that) and soon found myself back on the plateau where I was greeted with that warming smile I had now got used too. Dancing Cloud was sitting in the same place as before with the others sat around him within the stone circle in front of the fire as he beckoned me once again to join him. I sat with him and before I could think, I was given the peace pipe once again to draw on and within moments I was running through the forest through the eyes of a timber wolf negotiating every tree and bush with ease. I came upon a clearing where the sea lapped against the shore and I could smell the salt air blowing off the waves. Suddenly I noticed a young girl dressed in Indian clothing, collecting shells on the beach and when she turned I recognised her as the same girl I had shared the rostrum with at the first spiritualist church circle I attended a while ago, which was a surprise. I bounded off into the woods and then past houses and along the streets of a big city which I recognised as my own, but soon I was back on the plateau with Dancing Cloud holding my shoulders with his firm grip and looking into my eyes as he started to speak,

"The eyes of the timber wolf will guide you along your journey down on your earthly plane and you can call on him if you need his help at any time in the future". I felt quite comforted by the thought and I now had eagle and timber wolf guides along with Dancing Cloud himself. I thanked him and I was back in my chair in the sun lounge with the Native American flute music still playing. Moments later, I felt very refreshed I must say and more fascinated than ever about my journey and what the future could hold working with spirit.

The door went and in came Lesley from work and I told her all about the day's adventures and half an hour later she still had her coat on. The next evidence of spiritual manipulation came as soon as that evening when we decided to order a pizza as we both fancied staying in as we were tired. It was about eight o'clock when we heard a car pull up outside and then the doorbell rang. I answered the door and to my surprise a young lady was standing there who I instantly recognised as the same girl I had worked the rostrum with and seen in my meditation that very same afternoon. I could not believe my eyes as I had not seen her since that night so long ago and didn't know how to get in touch with her. She said,

"It's Pete isn't it? I've been trying to find you for some time now but nobody knew where you were,"

I replied, "I was only thinking about you this afternoon after a meditation session". She was delivering pizzas and it was her first night. Before I could say anything else she carried on, " I've been having strange dreams where I keep seeing an Indian Chief and beside him are both of us", this was all getting too much for me now and I went on to explain about my meditation during the afternoon and she was as gobsmacked as I was. Neither of us could get our heads around this so called chance meeting, but she had to go as she had more pizzas to deliver so I jotted down her number on a menu and she left as confused as I was. I have never been in touch with her since but I know she has developed into a good medium and hopefully we will meet up again one day. Mind blowing was the only way I could describe that whole particular day and I don't feel it was a coincidence, but spirit working at its best. When I go back to see Dancing Cloud she is always there with him and he has told me since that she is my sister and we have experienced amongst other things standing on rocks spear fishing for salmon together.

It was the following day

I can't move on without telling you first about this other incident that occurred when I was working in a popular nightclub in the city as a grill chef. Shortly after I left the Halls many years ago I had got to know some of the bouncers and bar girls very well and one day a few of us decided we would attempt to make our way around Europe fruit picking for a couple of years. Plans were drawn up and the leaving date was set and I was very excited about this adventure.

A job became available at the halls of residence as I explained earlier and I thought I would go for it anyway as the money was ok and you could live in as well and it would offer some stability in my life at that time but I was half hoping I wouldn't get it as I really fancied the European adventure but after the interview I was offered the position and I took it - much to the disappointment of my workmates who were really looking forward to us going around Europe. Anyway, they went without me and we had a good party before they left to see them on their way but deep down I still wished I was going with them.

I settled down to my new job and you know the rest, but a friend and myself decided that we would go away for Christmas and preferably to somewhere warm so we chose Spain for a week. I did not hear anything from the guys and girls and wondered how they were getting on and where they might be and what would have happened if I had gone with them. We flew out a week before Christmas and when we arrived at our destination the first thing I had to do was buy a coat as it was freezing and I had not gone prepared for cold weather by any means. In the hotel was an indoor pool which looked quite inviting and I fancied a swim so armed with a towel I made my way towards it and in my hurry I did not test the water first and dived straight into something that resembled the Arctic Ocean! I had instant brain freeze and became totally disorientated but I managed to find my way to the steps as quickly as I could and got out but I was sure I could hear tittering coming from folk around the pool and as you may have gathered was not heated and I'm surprised it didn't have ice on it! This was not really the start to the holiday I had dreamed of and after a few drinks at the bar I soon started to warm back up before we headed for the welcome meeting. The meeting took place in another hotel down the road and the cold wind was incredible as we made our way toward it. The trips on offer did not appeal to us with the exception of one to Gibraltar that we booked on right away as we didn't want to miss out and that was on Christmas Eve, which seemed a bit strange being the holiday period. The wind had dropped when we left the other hotel and made our way back to ours while taking a short cut along the beach and after a few too many drinks while at the welcome meeting we were a little loud should we say. As we were coming off the beach still in a light hearted mood we both noticed a member of the Spanish Police force with a rifle in his hands that he had trained on us which killed the mood a bit. We soon fell silent and a little scared as we came off the beach, still with the rifle trained on us we climbed the steps towards the hotel. We really hadn't got a clue what to do at this point but all I could think of was to walk past the guard and wish him a "good night" and it worked as he acknowledged us and finally lowered his rifle much to our relief. We stayed in the bar of the hotel that night for obvious reasons though I really didn't fancy a swim. We were about the two youngest blokes in the resort and that was possibly why we were targeted as we noticed everyone else seemed to be quite a bit older than ourselves.

I was really looking forward to our trip to Gibraltar and when Christmas Eve came around I was up early, showered and down for a hearty breakfast that turned out to be continental (I always feel short changed by them) but nothing could dampen my spirits that particular morning for some reason. On the coach, we passed vineyards, orange and lemon orchards and some spectacular scenery that whiled away the time and I suddenly found myself thinking about my old workmates who had gone fruit picking around Europe. It was probably the first time as I was so wrapped up in my new job now. We finally arrived at the border between Spain and Gibraltar; with our passports at the ready we disembarked from the coach towards passport control and remember it was Christmas Eve. The guards on the gates actually seemed a little worse for wear and possibly under the influence (if you know what I mean). If I had had a picture of Mickey Mouse on my passport I probably would have been waved through with no questions asked. Now we had the large expanse of runway to cross before we hit the town. Gibraltar was bustling with folk of all nationalities and the sun was hot right now as we passed street cafes and shops you would see on the high street back home any day of the week. There were gift shops by the score with very little variation in each but I managed to buy some presents for folk back home and Lesley of course, as we were now an item. As we walked down the main road I heard someone shout,

"Pete", I ignored it as who in hell would be calling me here but then I heard it again and as I turned round I was greeted by four of the friends I was supposed to have been travelling around Europe with and what were the chances of that I ask you! You could have knocked me down with a feather and for once in my life I was totally speechless for a while. After some hugs and kisses we headed for something to eat and a catch up about all that had been going on with them since we last met. It turned out that all six of them had settled in Spain now and lived in a typically Spanish town just across the border called La Linea and they wanted to show us their apartment and the town. I explained about the coach trip we were on but they were insistent we stayed and that they would drive us back on Christmas Day, so we readily agreed. Then one of them said,

" Only last night were we saying wouldn't it have been nice if Pete could have been here to share Christmas with us and here you are, it's unbelievable and you wouldn't believe it if you read it in a book", but you are.

We spent the day being shown the sights of Gibraltar by my friends and if you've never been its amazing and only fourteen miles across the water to Morocco. As Christmas Eve started to draw in we made our way back to La Linea and what a delight the place was and folk seemed very festive as we were to find out, as sleep would be out of the question. Back at the apartment (which was very nice may I add) we were subjected to an in depth account of all the European fruit picking experiences they had all been through and I can't say I wasn't a little jealous again. Two of the girls were out of town for Christmas and one of them had been a very close friend of mine back home so that was a little disappointing for me but she had met a Spanish lad so I hope it worked out for her. Earlier, on the way back over the border, it must have been the friendliest passport patrol I have ever been through with an alcoholic drink being offered to one and all and Christmas kisses for the girls - not like the patrol officer the other night who was itching for an excuse to shoot us. We all had a lovely evening putting the world to rights and then at midnight everything changed as Spanish folk poured out of their houses and into the streets. There were drums beating along with singing and dancing as a procession lead by a man in robes carrying a cross snaked its way through the narrow streets and more and more people joined this religious conga. Groups of folk were letting off fireworks, the bangs echoed through the narrow streets so there was nothing for it but to join in with all the festive frivolity going on down below. It was awesome and a scene I will never forget and so different from Christmas Eve back home which for me was a midnight communion, home for a cup of coffee and then off to bed. This was an all night celebration make no mistake, and the streets seemed to be filling up even more and at one point a group of about twenty guys came up to us and I feared the worst but all they said was,

"English, Merry Christmas" and after breathing a sigh of relief we all shook hands and they went on their merry way. We could learn a lot from the Spanish ways of doing Christmas but with dawn fast approaching thoughts turned towards getting back to our hotel further up country.

My friends kept their word and next day after some long goodbyes one of them drove us back to our hotel but I can't remember much as I was so tired but still elated. What were the chances of meeting up with them as timings had to be perfect for all parties concerned and as the saying goes 'spirit moves in mysterious ways'.

We returned to England the next day in the dead of night in temperatures of minus seventeen and the car boot lock was frozen solid which contained my nice warm sheepskin coat but nothing could dampen my spirits after that series of events.

Now back to where I was before, as I just wanted to make you aware of what spirit are capable of if you pray hard enough.

One evening when I had just got back from work I noticed a message had been left on the answer phone and I stopped what I was doing and started to listen. It was from Marian at the spiritualist church and could I ring her back as she would like to speak to me. I was excited by this and after my evening meal I rang her but there was no reply so I left a message and said that I would call by the church tomorrow as I had had a call out in that area and for Marian to ring me back if she wasn't going to be there. I heard nothing more and I only hoped she had picked up the message as I was now really looking forward to tomorrow. I had arranged my day so that once again I could be at the church for lunchtime but the morning threw me a few curve balls and it was now looking unlikely that I would make it as I had been called out of the area. Devastated, I headed back to my van but call it divine inspiration or whatever it was, my phone rang and it was the client that I had closest to the church and I suddenly felt spirit was not going to let me go that easily. I was a little later than I had hoped getting to the church but as I pushed the door to the church it opened and I made my way inside. As I climbed my way up the stairs to the small church I was met by a lovely lady and she was Marian, (now along time friend) who welcomed me in and before I knew it I had a cup of tea in my hand and a tin of biscuits in front of me. My hour was up before I knew it but we had had a lovely conversation and I had put her in the picture about my past and you know what that's been like so we arranged to meet up again so she could introduce me to a few people within the church.

The people I met where right up my alley and we all sang off the same hymn sheet (pun intended) and I began to feel more and more comfortable and it wasn't long until I found myself once again in a new circle along with Lesley.

In the mean time my heart skipped a beat when I answered the phone one evening and it was Caroline Clare on the other end of the line. She told me that things had gone badly wrong in France and she was now living in Ledbury Herefordshire and would we like to visit her so we could catch up again. My immediate response was,

"Yes of course we would", so it was arranged that we would drive up later that week.

The day came and a nice drive up to Ledbury was experienced by both of us and the town was beautiful and quite quaint to say the least. We soon after arrived at our destination, a small bungalow tucked away in a rural area of Herefordshire. Caroline gave us a great welcome in her own unique and inimitable style. Before I knew it I had a ring thrown at me and the words,

"What do you get from that Pete"? it was her Mother's ring and soon the energies were pouring off it and Caroline received a lovely message.

We decided to all go out to Upton-on-Severn after a cup of tea and we all had a lovely afternoon and it was awesome to be back in Caroline's company though I felt she was keeping something from me, call it my intuition. It was evening time when we finally said goodbye and started on our long journey home after a lovely day of conversation, laughter and tears.

Mum and Dad's Final Journey

My parents had both passed now and there was still the scattering of the ashes to be carried out and it wasn't as if we didn't know where this was to happen. They had drilled it into us for many years that there was one place and one place only and that was Cuckmere Haven near Seaford in East Sussex where they had carried out their courtship during the war years. It was also in their wills, so their plan was pretty fool proof and Mum had been waiting for only eighteen months for Dad to join her but now they were side by side in urns at the local funeral directors. It was up to Ron to collect them a couple of days before we were due to carry out the ceremony by the side of the river Cuckmere in I must agree a most beautiful part of the world which I had never seen before but parents were to give me a heads up before we even got there.

The river was tidal and if the ashes were to reach the sea the timing would have to be spot on and so everything would have to go like clockwork and if my parents had anything to do with it that would be the case.

The weekend soon came around and everyone was excited about what lay in store and a chance for family to meet up and reminisce about the old days when my parents ruled the roost. We were to stay with my sister and brother in law just outside Seaford in their trailer tent. We had been camping many times over the years and this was long before Lesley and myself discovered caravanning, so a trailer tent was a real luxury to us. Ron and Christine were to stay at a hotel in Seaford, no slumming it for them, and nieces and nephews were to join us later as and when.

It was a couple of days before the event as I was just going into a deep meditation with the Native American flute music softly playing in the background when I suddenly saw myself through the eyes of my spirit eagle surveying all below me and I was soaring over somewhere like the white cliffs of Dover and then following a meandering river slightly inland before alighting on a bridge over the river. Why here I thought to myself? There was a pavilion on one side of the river surrounded by lush green meadows and on the other side where bungalows with beautifully manicured gardens stretching down towards the river. I could smell the newly mown grass and I could hear children playing in the warm summer sunshine. It was an idyllic sight to behold and I could have stayed there for a lot longer but I was rudely awakened by the beating wings of the eagle as I rose and soared into the air low over a town. I caught a glimpse of the name Seaford on a signpost and then it suddenly clicked with me exactly what I had been shown. This was where the ashes were to be scattered that coming weekend, so when I was back in the sun lounge at home I grabbed a pen and a piece of paper and drew a map of what I had seen. I had never been there in my life, but spirit never lies, so I took it that that was what I would find when we finally got there, but there was a shock in store.

The drive down was a nightmare as we headed towards Dartford tunnel and it was a Friday afternoon with the words three-lane car park coming to mind. We eventually made it feeling a little worse for wear I might add. Lynne and David were already there and the smell of freshly grilled sausages and other bits and pieces was more than welcome at this particular juncture. During the evening, the rest of the clan started to arrive and a merry old time was had by all let it be said and by the time folk started to rise next morning some rather bleary eyes and sore heads were in evidence I'm afraid but it was an important day not only for us, but my parents as well. I could feel their energies from the moment I woke up as they were on a tight schedule and nothing was going to stand in their way. I could feel them getting more and more agitated as the day wore on and if anything went wrong now I would feel their wrath for sure (the advantages of being able to communicate with spirit) so this had to work. It was extremely windy but warm and dry as we relaxed outside the trailer tent as the tide would not be right until the late afternoon. All was going well until my brother in law decided he needed some piece of equipment from Eastbourne, which wasn't exactly just round the corner and the jungle drums as the saying goes started to beat loudly as it was now early afternoon and we were on a very tight schedule. This was going to throw a real spanner in the works and I knew it, but what could I do?

All of a sudden I heard,

"Pete fix it", a bit blunt I thought but I could see their point of view and then I heard,

"Tell him to go tomorrow, it's open then", so I tried it and after a conversation with Lynne it was agreed that that's what he would do. Thank goodness for that as my parents seemed to back off a little at that point. We all left en masse for Cuckmere and eventually found somewhere to park and as we got out of the cars we were all nearly blown inside out with the constant stiff wind. We made our way towards the river following the signposts and eventually we came upon a bridge and, guess what, it looked exactly the same as the one I had seen during my meditation. Something was wrong though. The pavilion was on the wrong side of the river as were the bungalows with the well manicured gardens and there was nowhere to scatter the ashes from the bridge because we would have all ended up looking like chimney sweeps. This was a real dilemma as the tidal river was pushing through strongly now so we were within our window of opportunity for the scattering if they were to make it to the sea as was my parent's wishes. I asked them for help and suddenly I was down the riverbank and walking the path at the side of the now turbulent river with the entourage following closely behind but the wind was still blowing strongly and the end result would still be the same. Suddenly we came to a bend in the river with an undercut on the far bank and believe it or not it was shielded from the severe wind somewhat - so this was to be the place where they would leave us on their journey to the sea. Ron had a CD player with a rendition of

"Danny Boy" on it, which was played while the ashes mixed together in the washing machine of a river that was now a muddy chocolate brown and very different from when we had stood on the bridge. It was a sombre occasion for all of us and there wasn't a dry eye amongst us but Mum and Dad had had their last request carried out so I felt we had done them proud when Ron suddenly shouted,

"Have you got the map Pete you drew during your meditation",

I replied "Yes it's in my back pocket", so I retrieved it and passed it to him and he opened it, took one look and said,

"Look! The map's right when you stand here", and sure enough it was. It was exactly right in every detail and from that I realised that we were meant to be where we were currently standing and I breathed a sigh of relief. After a short period of silence and a prayer we made our way back to the bridge where the wind was howling through the green iron bars like a demented banshee. We couldn't follow the river to the sea so it was back to the cars and a quick dash to a car park above Cuckmere Haven. I was beginning to see why my parents had wanted to have their ashes scattered in this place as it was breathtaking as we met up with the river once again which was down below us as it neared the white chalk cliffs before spewing out into the sea and mixing with the deep blue ocean that glistened in the early evening sun. It was beautiful and a picture I would have loved to have hung on the wall back home as a reminder of Mum and Dad forever. I felt as we clambered down the steep cliff path to the estuary that Mum and Dads ashes where already there and as I looked out to sea I saw a familiar sight. It was Mum and Dad with their backs towards me and holding hands above the sea before turning and waving with big smiles on their faces before fading away, which I relayed to all present. They had had their last request carried out and we could do no more for them now except wish them well in what they were doing spirit side of life.

We were hungry so we decided to go to a pub for an evening meal but on arrival the car park was very full and noisy so we thought better of it and headed for Seaford itself. There was a lovely little café that I was being drawn to, so Ron, Christine, Lesley and myself decided to get something to eat as it had been quite a while now and the hunger pangs were becoming quite evident. As we sat down at the small rickety table with solid wood chairs that grated as they slid across the stone floor it felt a little uncomfortable to me and I wanted to sit where Lesley was sitting and not for the first time you may remember from previous escapades. We swapped seats but you would have thought she'd have learnt her lesson by now but as usual there was a reason because as I looked up there was an original water colour painting of Cuckmere Haven in all its beauty on a similar day as today. I had to have it. If I had been sitting in Lesley's seat I probably would never have seen it. A reasonably large amount of money changed hands but I was happy with my purchase and I'm sure my parents had more than a little to do with it. Armed with my newly acquired painting we made our way back to the car and to try and find the others who had decided on fish and chips but when we had seen the queue we had thought better of it. They had only just started their meals when we arrived back after our hearty fayre in the olde worlde café so we decided to take Ron and Christine back to their hotel and a little bit of luxury - not that Lynne and David's hospitality was not enjoyable. As we pulled up in the hotel car park we arranged to ring them later that evening but they were to ring much sooner than that, as I will now explain. Ron and Christine had gone into the foyer of the hotel and noticed an array of postcards, old and new, that were being laid out for the next day and had not been there earlier, so as avid collectors they decided to take a look at what was on offer. It was then Ron caught a glimpse of a card and painted on the front of it was a picture of the exact spot where we had eventually scattered Mum and

Dad's ashes earlier that day hence why he phoned me back so quickly. It wasn't even that much of a picturesque spot on the river and there where much nicer scenes to paint but there it was in all its glory, which was nothing short of amazing. Coincidence? No. Spiritual manipulation? Definitely yes, and we still can't get our heads around it to this day. Spirit does work in mysterious ways as the saying goes.

Learning to Trust in Spirit

Back at the spiritualist church things were going well and I was getting to see and talk to some very interesting mediums and I was in my element. The circle was going well now and the evidence I was bringing through was getting stronger the more I practiced and Lesley was doing pretty well too. We had been through a quite intense session and I was quite happy with my evening's efforts when I noticed a text on my phone when we were having a cup of tea with friends upstairs and it was from my sister Lynne.

It read, "Hi Pete can you give me a ring as soon as possible as I need to ask you a favour", ominous I thought to myself, and it puzzled me all the way home. I rang her when we arrived back and she told me that she had a good friend who was having a few issues and would it be possible for me to give her a reading one weekend which shocked me a little because I hadn't really been let loose on the public before but I'd have to do it sometime. So I readily agreed and a date was arranged on the spot. It was to be that coming weekend, so not too long to bite my fingernails down to the bone, but I was also rather excited at the same time so mixed emotions really. The day came and I really wasn't trusting in myself and I felt that I would be hung out like a fish to dry which many mediums have experienced in their early days i'm sure, but there was no harm in trying and I had to fight these personal demons. We arrived at Lynne's well before lunch which gave us a chance to have a chat and a welcome cup of coffee and for my nerves to settle but while I was sitting there I started to picture a little blond haired boy with curly hair tentatively making his way towards me and he was holding something in his hand which I really did not recognise, other than it was made of wood, long and pointy at one end and thicker and blunter at the other. He told me his name was John but I had guessed that as my sister had lost a little boy with the same name shortly after his birth but what was he holding? He told me his Mummy had made it for him and I relayed this to my sister who looked at me open mouthed. She disappeared very quickly and I thought what have I done? when She suddenly reappeared with the same object the little boy had been trying to give me. She told me it was a lace bobbin that I was being shown and that she had just acquired one which she had had inscribed with the name John in the memory of her little boy now passed to spirit. We both had a tear in our eye at this precise moment and I could not have made this up as I knew nothing about it and lace making wasn't really my thing anyway. I thanked spirit who, before he disappeared, told me that he was well and being looked after by other members of the family spirit side and for Mummy and Daddy not to worry. I was not expecting this but my trust in spirit had gone up a notch as it always seems to when you start to build a communication and I couldn't now wait to be introduced to Lynne's friend down the road.

We decided to have lunch after we had been to see Lynne's friend down the road and as we knocked on the door I could feel those nagging doubts creeping in once again even though I had just had an amazing experience. After introductions, I sat on the sofa and started to bring forward a big man, quite an imposing figure who was blowing a whistle and was dressed as a referee. This was verified by my client so that was a good start and my confidence was now growing as a result. I knew spirit wouldn't let me down and why would they anyway as it may be the only chance that person would have of getting a message through to a loved one. As the reading progressed, some family difficulties were unearthed which the father and granddad to her children was not happy about and came out with some stark revelations that she did not know about but had a feeling they might be happening. All was going well but I felt there was something more that she needed from the reading that I hadn't given her. I was not aware that she had been praying to her Dad earlier that day and to prove validation beyond all reasonable doubt she had asked him to use a trigger word but as yet that had not been revealed. After the reading which had gone well she went into the kitchen to make a drink before we left and while I was looking towards the kitchen door which was open I could see fluffy clouds floating about and as she came out of the kitchen with a cold glass of water for me (something I always have during a spirit communication) I casually said to her,

"I know this is strange but I keep seeing magenta coloured clouds floating around you in the kitchen", and I got a different type of reaction to the one I had expected,

"Pete, Magenta is the trigger word we had devised between us for the validation I needed, thank you, thank you", and put her arms around me and tears of joy started to flow. I was now elated and I thanked her Dad and the spirit side of life for working with me and we left. Back for a well earned french stick, pate and crisp lunch which was washed down with a nice hot cup of tea and all was well with the world right now on both sides of the ether.

Near Lynne's were a couple of good cold water fish dealerships and Lesley and myself love our koi carp and keep them at home so any opportunity we can grab we will take and this afternoon was to be no exception. So, after lunch and still on a high, we headed to the dealerships where I hoped we could find some more beautiful Japanese koi for our pond and we are very picky when it comes to choosing these awesome fish. The first site was very busy and it was hard to see into the vats so a little frustrated we moved on to the other dealer nearby and it was much quieter there and some of the fish were pure quality and yes they were expensive but we were happy to pay for them. There were some beauties at astronomical prices which would have required a mortgage near enough to purchase but surprisingly there were quite a few gems that were in our price range. Their colours were so bright they looked like an artist's pallet with their markings. We have kept koi for many years now so we know what we are after. We both have to agree on a fish as we will both have to look at it day after day and we would be parting with a reasonable amount of money. There is something about koi that is so spiritual and I can watch them for hours gliding gracefully around the pool, morning, noon or night and that won't change. If it hadn't been for the purchase of some beautiful koi holding us up from leaving later that evening, my niece would not have received her reading from a friend in spirit. We bought two beautiful koi, which still swim around with the others in our pool to this day, and headed back to my sister's for tea rather later than expected. We had to stay later as it would have been sacrilege not to help Lynne out with her spaghetti bolognaise and it did not disappoint.

Jenny is Lynne and David's youngest daughter and at this time she was going through her own grieving period, following the passing of her good friend so she was very quiet which was unlike Jenny who was usually the life and soul of the party. I felt troubled to see her like this and wished there was something I could do to ease her mind so I sat with her just to have a reassuring chat when I noticed a girl appear beside her dressed a bit like a Goth but I had a feeling it was her friend who had come to ease her mind. I described to Jenny what she looked like and the clothes she was wearing and I then told her she was smiling and telling her not to worry as she was safe and nothing could have been done to save her. Jenny recognised her straight away as her friend and she suddenly became open and started to tell me about their times together. Jenny's friend then went on show me masses of pink roses and I began to hear a well known pop chart hit in my head and when I relayed these incidents to Jenny she said,

"Pete, they were all things we thought she would like at her funeral, does she say she liked them", her friend smiled at this and gave the thumbs up signal so that was ok then. Then she held up a mobile phone, waved it at me and proceed to take the sim card out of it but why I thought to myself so I told Jenny this and I will always remember her reply,

"OMG how can you know that, I've told nobody as it was a personal thing for my friend", once again spirit had excelled as they had earlier in the day with the bobbin and the 'Magenta' clouds. Jenny went on to say that while she was at Chapel of Rest visiting her friend for the last time, she quietly slipped a brand new sim card in her friend's pocket and said the words,

"That's in case, when you reach the other side if there is any way you can get a message through to me please do and this might just help", Jenny pushing the boundaries as usual bless her. We both had tears in our eyes at this point as it was just so moving and why I do this knowing that I have reconnected someone with a loved one, be it a friend or a complete stranger. I've never seen such a change in Jenny in such a short space of time as she was more or less back to her old self and then she started to bombard me with questions to ask her friend which were personal to them and that's were I will leave it. If it hadn't been for us purchasing those lovely koi, I don't think Jenny would have received her message at that time.

What of the koi, I hear you ask. Haven't they have been in the car for ages by now? Not at all as we are always very professional when it comes to koi. They were purchased in large water filled thick doubled up plastic bags with oxygen pumped in and enough for twelve hours travelling time, then placed in large polystyrene boxes with lids and then put in the back of the car for the journey. The boxes were removed from the car at Lynne's house and placed in a cool shaded area until we were ready to leave. We never leave animals to suffer in the heat and that includes fish, birds and anything else that God has created. After our lovely meal and a good chat it was time to leave and head homeward and now it was cooler for the koi as well. As we drove round the corner, I started to get serious hair tickling telling me spirit was about and it was

Jenny's friend's house we were passing. We arrived back home safely an hour and a half later and removed the koi from the car straight away and carried them to the pool, then took them from the boxes but left them to float for an hour of so to acclimatise to the possible differing water conditions and went inside for a well earned cup of tea. Sometime later, when it was getting cooler and darker, we slipped our new additions into the pool where they still swim many years later with the others. What a day that was I thought to myself, three readings, two of which were unintentional, but spirit knew different, some very happy folk along the way and with two well fed and happy koi keepers.

I couldn't wait for the next morning to go and greet my new koi who showed no ill effects from the previous days journey and were just as hungry as the others when it came to the usual feeding frenzy. As I went down the stairs I noticed an answerphone message again but that could wait until I had fed my beauties and when I eventually did it was from an old friend who needed me to do a reading for her Mother. After the previous days success, I rang her back and agreed to do it as what could surprise me now I thought.

The lady in question was one I had met through dog training and it all happened after repeatedly seeing ghosts in the training centre and she was also a very good dog trainer but it wasn't her I had come to do the reading for. It was her Mother, an elderly lady but in very good health for her age and her hospitality was second to none as we were offered regular hot drinks and cakes. The reading began and the usual suspects made their presence known which is always nice and helps put people at ease but a little lady with a fur coat and stoll round her neck was trying to butt in and she was waving a suitcase to get my attention. The lady I was reading for knew who it was but didn't give anything away and I'm sure she would have been good at poker as she was expressionless but this was to change. She asked me who I thought it was and it felt like her

Grandma and so it turned out to be and this was the one person she had wanted to know had passed safely to spirit for a long time. Then she said,

"Can you see what she is doing",

I said "Yes she is standing by the side of a docks in her fur coat with a suitcase beside her and she is about to board a very large old ship",

"Yes" she said,

"Carry on" but how could I say it looked like the 'Titanic', I would be run out of town for sure or could it be I wondered as I had always been taught by Caroline to say what you see. I tried to connect with her Grandma when in front of my eyes I saw the words 'Lusitania', the 'Titanic's', sister ship and that was blessed relief let me tell you so I continued,

"Your Grandmother was about to board the 'Lusitania to America" and it was a good validation.. "She has come though to tell you she is ok on the spirit side of life and still watches over you, but also has been moving objects about in your house and you guessed correctly who it was". Suddenly my client got up and left the room with tears in her eyes but she soon came back clutching an old photograph in a wooden frame and handed it to me, still visibly shaken and the picture portrayed her Grandmother standing on the dockside in her fur coat and stoll by the side of the 'Lusitania' before emigrating to America many years ago and I was quite taken aback.

She said,

"No one knows about this, only family and even my daughter doesn't know she went via the 'Lusitania', I'm amazed that no one has brought her through before for me and it's what I have been waiting for for so long". I thought to myself, probably because they didn't want to mention the 'Titanic' and I was glad I hadn't had to either. That was it after that, as nothing else mattered to her anymore and she was more than happy with her reading and even offered me a considerable quantity of money which I flatly refused as spirit had given the message freely and I was just glad to bring some closure for this lovely lady.

Back at the Spiritualist Church our circle had ran its course and I was left thinking to myself, what happens next as I was now developing and working well with spirit and I didn't want to jeopardise that in any way so a course of action was needed.

I had written poetry for a number of years and had quite a collection and I decided I should share it with the world and very soon my first published book was in my hands and a very proud moment indeed in my life. It had an awesome bright cover and was titled 'You're Having a Larf, ' fun poetry for all the family and people who have bought it readily agree including the church who have started using some of the renditions in their sermons before demonstrations and quite often laughter can be heard and smiling faces seen among the congregation which is what it was all about really, bringing some happiness into peoples lives. It was after one such demonstration that Marian approached me and said,

"There is a new closed circle starting in the next few weeks on a Monday night and I'm inviting yourself and Lesley to join and it will be run by a lady called Norma who is very good at what she does and I think it will be right up your street", and this got me excited as one door had closed and another one had just apparently been opened.

Ghost Hunting back on the Agenda

With everything that had been going on I really hadn't been doing any ghost hunts and I was starting to be bitten by the bug again. I had started a new job and that was allowing me into places I could only really dream of regarding investigations, such as old railway stations, stately homes and of course inns, but it was a castle that was to be next on the agenda perched high on a hill in Staffordshire. Lesley and I had been there numerous times on day visits and had picked up on strange phenomena so when I saw they were advertising overnight ghost hunts with evening meal and breakfast at a very reasonable price may I add, so we set the ball rolling. I sent the word out to family and friends and very soon all the places had been filled including two for my current boss and his wife so I was praying that it all went well.

We arrived on the night and the sky was a carpet of stars as we looked down into the valleys of Derbyshire bathed in moonlight and already it felt a little eerie with the turrets pointing their way up to the heavens and the ruined castle silhouetted against the night sky. You could just imagine soldiers in armour clanking around the place and various varieties of livestock wandering about at will but what was in store was a little more sinister than that.

Everybody had turned up which was pleasing and we all sat down to eat a very appetising and filling three course meal while much talk echoed around the tables of what might be in store during the nights events. There was entertainment laid on by our host and by the time that had finished I glanced at my watch and it was past eleven o'clock already so I gathered the troops up and we began our investigation in the Great Hall and surrounding areas, the part of the castle that remains intact to this day. There was one reputably bad energy in this area and he would quite often make his presence felt in a manner of different ways and tonight would be no exception as we were about to find out. As it was such a known paranormal area we all piled into the Kings Bedroom but the lights were left on for safety reasons and with so many of us in there it was probably a good idea as well. We were all stood in rows listening to tales about this area from a guide when my boss's wife let out a blood-curdling scream and slid down the wall and crumpled in a heap on the floor motionless. Some of us grabbed hold of her and carried her out of the bedroom, down the stairs and into the fresh air followed by Lesley my wife who, through experience, knew how to deal with psychic attacks. It was quite a few minutes later that she started to come round mumbling to herself and we all drew a collective sigh of relief. She didn't seem to really know where she was at first but eventually she began to tell us what had happened. She said,

"I was standing with the rest of you, when what appeared to be a very large black shadow made its way around the wall and stood in front of me, pushed a large hand into my face and the next thing I could remember was coming too outside, under the stars. Remember this was my bosses' wife we are talking about and I had a feeling my employment status was on very thin ice at this precise moment but it only seemed to encourage them to try and experience more much to my great relief. People had broken off into their own little groups now and were exploring the dungeons, steps up the towers and anywhere else the paranormal could be hiding while a few of us stayed in the Great Hall. I soon picked up on a little girl called Ellie who would move objects and chairs about when nobody was looking and then show herself as a spirit light more or less on command. Some of the photos were really good with orbs being captured left right and centre and small snippets of EVP were also caught. Some mists were captured as well in the dungeons that couldn't be explained along with stones being thrown at some of the party but the highlight was my boss's wife's experience in the king's bedroom. We all slept where we could on chairs, the floor and some didn't sleep at all and breakfast was a really welcome sight at six thirty the following morning.

I kept my job, you will be glad to hear, but my boss was to be replaced soon after with a man who, let's just say, was a sceptic of the highest order. I was not allowed to mention anything to do with ghosts or the paranormal at work and definitely not to any of my clients, as if I would, but how could I not mention it when I was standing in a school kitchen when a large heavy double pan rack appeared to roll along in front of our eyes and the pans started rattling like an earthquake was going on, you tell me? At a meeting of the school kitchens a few months later the Area Catering Manageress relayed this story to my new boss and it wasn't long before I got my ears burned, thanks spirit. Perhaps I couldn't do anything paranormal at work, though I still did occasionally, readings mostly as it happened but it wasn't going to stop me outside of work that was for sure.

Ron and Christine had been on a day excursion to an Abbey in Nottinghamshire and had experienced some really strange stuff while they were there that they could just not explain, so they invited Lesley and myself to spend an afternoon with them at the same place to see what we could pick up on. As it was we had nothing planned for the weekend and being the height of summer there was no football to hold us back and so we arranged to meet them at the Abbey that Sunday.

It was a beautiful day and very hot as I remember and more people were outside than in the Abbey as you would probably expect with any chance of a suntan gratefully snapped up. Ron and Christine had already arrived and were having a cup of tea in the café so we went to join them. As we walked into this area I could see the image of a young lad leading a horse along in front of me before disappearing through a brick wall and when I mentioned this to Ron he didn't seem very surprised. He told me that this had been the old stable block and where the stable boy and horse had disappeared used to be an entrance to the stable yard so I was quite pleased to get validation once again. After some refreshments we all decided to visit the grounds as it was such a beautiful day and that we would leave the Abbey itself until later and the large lake across the wide lawns was drawing me anyway, not surprising as anything that might contain fish usually would be my first port of call. I peered into the fairly clear shallow water, quite close to where a heron was standing motionless, and only its head darting forward into the lake gave its position away as it stalked its fishy prey. It must have been a better fisherman than me, because I couldn't see anything that resembled a fish, but what I could see were ships and (yes you are reading it right), ships and small battleships at that, which were firing on each other with cannons. These appeared to be scale models of battleships from centuries ago with various coloured sails that actually were destroying each other in front of my eyes but I had to be imagining this surely. I passed this information on to the rest of our party and received some rather funny looks I must say, which didn't make me feel any better during my moment of madness or so I thought. Nothing else of any significance happened in the grounds besides getting lost in the maze that Lesley had suggested we try but if you have ever seen her with a jigsaw puzzle, to her this maze was a piece of cake but I on the other hand beg to differ! It was eventually time to explore the abbey and so we made our way inside where it was very much cooler and as we paid our admission fees I could not help but notice a woman in a long flowing dress gliding down the stairs in our direction. It was a long and wide sweeping staircase and as Ron took a photograph a bright orb was captured right in the middle, which was probably her. Next we entered into a large hall with tapestries adorning the walls when I felt my hand being held, which rather reminded me of the children at the Inn on the Moor but it was only one hand this time so I began to try and bring this person forward. It turned out to be a little boy dressed in a blue tunic and buttoned up to the top and he certainly was not modern in any way and he pointed in the direction of a small drum on a windowsill, which was roped off along with an old wicker style chair next to it. As I approached this area with Ron following closely behind busily snapping away with his camera hoping to catch something paranormal, we both froze as we clearly heard the drum beat six times in a loud rhythmic fashion and then stop as suddenly as it had started. We looked at each other in total disbelief and tried to find a logical explanation for this phenomenon, but none could be found, even after jumping up and down on the floor, open and closing doors and treading on any uneven floorboard we could find. The little boy was still with me and I knew it was him that had banged the drum as he grinned once more and then ran off and disappeared not to be seen again on our visit. When the girls finally caught up with us a short while later, they had their own tale to tell about hearing footsteps on the corridor which was why they had been delayed but I think Ron and I would rather have experienced the beating drum given the choice. Nothing else happened for a while, but when it did again, it came as a surprise along one of the corridors that was lined with paintings and all four of us were to witness it and it came in the form of a wet dog smell (which was very strong I might add) and having kept dogs at home the smell was very familiar to me. We all smelt it and all of us agreed it was definitely wet dog and at this time the corridor floor was covered with raffia matting and then we heard what could only be described as dog toenails on concrete coming along the corridor and suddenly stop. Where they stopped was right below a large portrait of a Newfoundland dog that had belonged to a previous owner and the smell had now dissipated completely as well which we found very strange. We moved on, wondering what would happen next, when we came to a large room with beautiful furnishings and a huge long heavy wooden table, which felt quite inviting. There were some chairs dotted around the edge of the room and I chose to sit down on one for a few moments and really I don't remember what happened next but apparently my voice became very much deeper and I was heard to shout,

"You have no right to be in here, leave before I have you thrown to the dogs",

I carried on,

"How dare you disturb my peace and quiet, go now",

I don't remember any of it but apparently an evil Lord had taken over me and I had to be calmed down. Later that day we were to find out that in the room I had been in, women were banned, and this was how it would have been at those times.

We soon came across some side rooms, which contained some very interesting artefacts as we were to find out but I had to get through the doors first as it was as if an invisible barrier was preventing me from going in. Every time I tried to enter one particular room I began to feel sick and dizzy and I would have to back off to allow myself to regain my composure before trying again. At about the fifth attempt I finally made it, which was quite a battle, and I still didn't feel right but I was in now and I had to find out what was causing this discomfort. There was a large glass cabinet in the middle of the room that had a sword displayed in it and I realised that this was my nemesis and the reason I could not stay in here for any length of time as it had been used by one of the Lords to kill his uncle with. While I was looking at the sword, Lesley took a picture which seemed to show the clear outline of a bear on the back of my jacket which I imagine was one of my spirit animal protectors looking after my welfare. I was very glad to get out of that room I must tell you, and the doom and despondency seemed to lift from my shoulders as I did. My spirits would be raised even higher a few minutes later as Ron who had gone into the next side room suddenly called me. He had found an article with sketches of mock sea battles having been performed on the lake and I could now not believe what I was looking at and once again my trust in spirit had been strengthened. I really had thought at the time that over active imagination was playing a very large part in what I had experienced but nothing could have been further from the truth. There it was in black and white in front of my eyes. This was turning out to be an extraordinary afternoon and I really wasn't expecting anything else when we passed by the nursery on the way out. Out of the corner of my eye, I saw a woman standing to one side of a grandfather clock in the hallway and she was wearing a grey uniform and her features were quite prominent along with the strange shaped hat on her head. (I would like to explain at this point that when I see spirit they come through as a mental image which gradually builds in strength but on occasions I have seen three-dimensional figures as in the old fisherman in Greece but this is a very unusual occurrence) As we climbed the stairs I had a spider like attack on the top of my head which was caused by a build up of energy and something I have experienced many times before as you already know. As I was scratching my head to rid myself of this feeling my eyes were drawn to a portrait on the staircase wall and there before me was the same woman I had seen by the grandfather clock earlier who turned out to be the children's nanny. Once I had acknowledged her the cobwebbing instantly stopped as if it never been there in the first place.

It was now getting late in the afternoon as we made our way back to the warmth outside when we passed the member of staff Ron had spoken to about me on his previous visit because of my ability to see ghosts. Ron introduced me to the person in question and he was more than interested to hear what I, along with the others, had experienced on our visit. I asked him what would be the chance of doing a night investigation in the Abbey thinking I was about to be chased down the road for asking such an impertinent question, but his response was very surprising to all of us. He told us to write down our details and that he would get back to us with any updates and I thought to myself that's the last we will hear from him but

I was to be proved wrong.

It was only a week later when my brother had a reply from the Abbey offering us an opportunity to investigate the site and once the word was out, it filled up very quickly with people I could vouch for including my ex boss and his wife. The individual price was fairly cheap and as we were just happy to have the chance to be investigating it and we were making no profit for ourselves, which sadly is not the case on many of these types of investigations that are run by groups now a days. We had to have tour guides on duty throughout the night, which was part of the deal as there were so many valuable artefacts about but this was not a problem and with everything in place we drew up our plans.

The night arrived and we were all to meet up at the gatehouse from where we were to be escorted to the abbey in convoy. As we travelled along the driveway you could see the moon reflecting off the lake and being broken up by the ripples in the stiff breeze, the whole site taking on a rather eerie ambience. Everybody had turned up and after a health and safety talk we began our vigil as there was no time to lose. I had brought my divining rods again so folk could see a communication in action and did not have to hear me drone on about what I was sensing and seeing. Almost immediately the rods sprung into life and pointed us in the direction of the library and to where we could find information about the lords who lived here in the past and soon it became clear that this communication was with a very well known and much renowned poet. For the rest of the night he led the way with the aid of the rods around the abbey but at one point in a bedroom a woman stepped in who must have been his wife as I started to hear her say,

"Get him to show you the elephants", which I repeated to all assembled and they must have thought I had gone bonkers. Where on earth would or why would there be elephants in this abbey. I went with it and she stayed with me without the use of the rods for a while still repeating the same words. But where could they be? I now had a good strong link with this lady and she was pointing me in certain directions until I rounded one corner and there to all our amazement was a large model cavalcade of elephants in a procession dressed in all their finery. A collective gasp could be heard from the group. She went on to say, that she had brought this back from Africa as a present for her husband and it was his favourite piece in the Abbey. We moved on down a corridor when suddenly she turned and went left through the wall and was gone but why had she turned there I wondered? One of the guides came up with the answer as where she had disappeared used to be the entrance into the dining room but had recently been blocked up, which made sense. The Lord was back now and he seemed to always be close to one of the female guides and on asking subconsciously he said he liked her and she reminded him of his wife and later talking to her she would tell me she had left working there three times but had kept coming back as she felt so comfortable in the place. Now she knew the reason why it brought a tear to her eye, but again, not one of sadness and as far as I know she is still working there. Orbs were being caught on cameras all over the place which kept people preoccupied and some had gone to other areas with guides to do their own thing. The last event that occurred that night was down in the cloisters where some candles in long tall holders were stood at either end of the wooden pews and when one of the group took a photograph it showed the candles as being lit and giving off plumes of smoke. So what? you say, until you realise that those candles were never lit for health and safety reasons and on everybody else's pictures they weren't lit either but a phenomenon that had been recorded before at the abbey that nobody has an explanation for.

 The end of the vigil came and everybody seemed to have had a good night and my ex bosses wife went home in one piece and if only they all could have experienced what the four of us did on our day visit, but that's ghost hunting for you.

Within a few days, I started to have some feedback regarding the abbey and a couple from Coventry who had been on a number of our investigations had been talking with their landlord about the abbey. He had asked them about inviting us to do an investigation at his Social Club as he was experiencing strange occurrences that he needed answers for. Of course I jumped at the chance and when I heard that there was a hot meal being laid on and if I acted as their medium for the night mine would be free, how could I resist.

Back at the Spiritualist Church, Norma's group had started in the lovely downstairs church with the beautiful stained glass windows which I can never get enough of, but as there were only twelve of us it felt a bit like a few marbles in a biscuit tin. After three weeks we were down to six members and then the circle seemed to settle into a comfortable place to be. It was like we were becoming a family that had met many times before though we had never cast eyes on one another before this circle. We did deep colour meditations and I'm sure I could write a book on my experiences during these sessions as they were amazing, but again, my mediumship development was not seemingly developing any further and if I wanted to be on the rostrum I would have to look elsewhere.

It was strange that the other four members of our circle all belonged to a dowsing group - something we were both very interested in resulting in our little family becoming closer still. We have investigated many varied and interesting places over recent times with the dowsing group and I think without our spiritual circle this adventure in our lives would not have come about.

Out of the blue Caroline Clare rang and that always filled me with joy but this time I sensed something was wrong and my intuition rarely is. Caroline was very ill and needed to see Lesley and myself fairly quickly as she had much to speak with us about. This sounded serious and as it was Friday we arranged to travel up the next day and I wondered what would be in store and I cant say I wasn't worried. We arrived in Ledbury around lunchtime the next day and her son met us at the door. Caroline was lying on the settee covered in a blanket and she looked very jaundiced and very different to the Caroline we had seen on our previous visit. Before we knew it she had struggled to her feet to hug both of us in turn. She told us she had cancer and nothing now could be done for her and that it was a matter of time but not too worry as when she passed she wouldn't leave me alone, typical Caroline bless her. We had heartfelt conversations during the day and I brought her mother through with a very valuable message which made her cry but not with sadness. The hospice nurse turned up and asked us if we could leave, very politely I might add as Caroline had done far more that day than she should have. Caroline looked very tired and smiled and waved at us as we said our goodbyes for the last time. We left details of how we could be contacted when the time came but I'm afraid those wishes were never fulfilled sadly. We made our way home with tears rolling down our cheek's as we knew her transition to spirit would not be long.

I woke up one September morning with the sun streaming through the bedroom curtains and Lesley had already left for work as her side of the bed was empty and her car was gone so she must have been quiet which I was grateful for. I could hear Samba, my faithful old black Labrador, scratching at the kitchen door and I must have woken him moving around on the floorboards upstairs. He was nicknamed 'the loveable rogue' because that was how he had been all through his years and would be until his dying day but his hips had started to go and he was in pain and his movements very slow now. I decided to take him down the local disused quarry line for a walk, which would take a long time in his current state, of that I was sure. He used to be such an athletic dog that could leap five barred gates and swim in the large swollen salmon rivers of Wales and we never feared for his safety and I even remember throwing his ball (he loved his ball) into the sea for him to fetch, but on this occasion he lost sight of it and just kept swimming out further into the distance and the nearest land was Ireland and we began to wonder. I threw a stone as far as I could and he heard the splash which diverted his attention back towards the shore and us but would he have kept going, we will never know. He had stolen sausages from people's barbecues while they were still cooking and landed us in all sorts of trouble but he was my boy and I seem to remember him running round next doors back garden with their prize cactus in his mouth devoid of its pot at one time. That was all a long time ago now and he was a shadow of his former self and it worried me that very soon he would no longer be with us. That day was closer than I knew. Off we went and once down the railway I unclipped his lead and he hardly moved where a few years ago he would have been off like a bat out of hell looking for anything that resembled another dog, however far away. We walked for a bit and then he lay down and just looked at me mournfully before eventually staggering to his feet but this happened twice more in the space of half a mile and on the final time I could see in his eyes that he had had enough and his time was near. I thought I could hear him saying,

"Dad its been fun but its time for me to go as I can't do this anymore", which brought a tear to my eye as I didn't want him to suffer and only wanted what was best for him, so our walk was cut short but it still took an age for us to get home and I'm glad it did as it was to be our last walk together down the railway. Lesley was home later that evening as she worked long shifts at the hospital and as she came through the door she could see that I was upset and asked me what was wrong. I explained about our walk and that I felt it was time for 'the loveable rogue' to be released from his pain and suffering. After much heart wrenching and soul-searching thinking are we doing the right thing, a decision was made to let him go. You wonder though - were we doing the right thing and this played havoc with me all night long and the next morning seemed to race round and then I was on the phone to the vets explaining the situation. The appointment was arranged for eleven am and at quarter to I carried Samba to the car for his last journey. Lesley was back at work and had said her goodbye's to Samba earlier and it was a very tearful occasion but something all dog lovers have to experience. At the vets, I was ushered straight into the back room so we didn't have to sit with the public and their cats and a dog which was a relief, though I don't think 'the loveable rogue' would have even noticed them. In the back room Samba (who hated the vets and many had the scars to prove it) seemed so calm and kept licking me. The vet offered an alternative but he couldn't guarantee it would be successful but Lesley and I had made up our minds and Samba needed his release. By the way, he was given the name Samba because when he was a puppy he used to gyrate his whole body when excited which reminded us of the rhythmical dance 'the Samba'. The vet left Samba and myself alone for a few minutes while he prepared the injection that would bring the old boy his peace so we had a hug and I asked Samba to find a way to get a message to me in a song on the radio or by some words I would overhear, to say he had safely passed to spirit and to let me know we had done the right thing as I was being eaten up inside right now. The vet came back in and asked me if I wanted to stay but I declined his offer. Suddenly Samba turned his head away from me and shut his eyes and I knew he was ready to go. I thanked the vet and left in tears as 'the loveable rogue' my old Samba was sent to the other side or so I hoped. It's like losing one of your family and I am not ashamed to say that I cried because I did and for some time to come and you will know that feeling if you have ever owned a pet.

It was about an hour later when I went to the local supermarket for some milk as I had been up so early and drank so much tea and coffee before and after the ordeal. The usual music was being piped into the store when I heard out of the blue the song 'I have a dream' and the words 'I believe in angels, when I know the time is right for me, I'll cross the stream, I have a dream' and so it continued and by the time the music had stopped I knew Samba had passed safely and we had done the right thing. I was elated and couldn't wait to tell Lesley when she got home but thinking about it now the store only played piped music and not songs, which made it all the more interesting for me.

Our friends who had arranged the ghost investigation at the Social Club in Coventry had finalised the details and it soon came around on a freezing cold night in mid November and I was glad we were to have a hot meal before we started. It wasn't far to go - only half an hour down the motorway but it was foggy and snow lay on the ground in a thin carpet, which made the journey quite treacherous so it took a little longer. As we pulled into the car park the building looked quite ominous and rather old with icicles hanging from the roof and window ledges like long tentacles or fingers on a bony withered hand and a shiver ran down my spine. Some of the others had now arrived and as the front door opened and light flooded out into the car park we got out of the car and crunched across the hard compacted snow, slipping and sliding as we went, both laughing as I did my famous Bambi on ice impersonation. Once inside the warmth hit you and my glasses instantly steamed up and I had to remove them to see where I was going and through my fuzzy vision that was not that easy. I tried to negotiate my way past tables and chairs towards the bar for a complimentary hot mixed spiced mulled wine. It all seemed very well organised but only knowing Lesley and our two friends it was a little overwhelming for us and as I was to be their guest medium for the night the pressure steadily mounted. The meal was lovely and anything and everything was talked about during the meal and all the party were in good spirits but a small few gave me the impression that they were out on a party night and not a serious investigation but they had paid their money so were entitled to be there (more the pity). Eventually things quietened down a bit and I explained a little about myself, what I did and what I expected from the night and after a quick guided tour by the landlord I felt the energies of the areas to investigate and we began. As the lights started to go off one by one the customary ghost noises and folk grabbing each other started just like an over grown kindergarten and I knew my first impressions had been right and especially from one young couple who I would have willingly tied to a lamp post in the bitter weather and returned to at the end of the vigil but you can't do that can you? As we approached the hallway I started to receive the impression of a cleaning lady who I made a clear connection with and as a visual aid for the group I also used the divining rods but there were sceptics among us, and unless a ghost jumped out and said "Boo," were not going to accept anything I said as being legitimate and yes it was the young couple I had taken an instant dislike to. Especially later on in the night when I found them using my divining rods to find out whether or not they would be having sex with each other later that night. I had visions of them trying it tied to that lamp post in the car park and had a little chuckle to myself. The cleaning lady was verified as a member of staff who had passed away recently but to some it was a lucky guess - even though I got her name and age right so I needed something to blow their socks off and spirit eventually obliged. Loads of orbs were being caught on cameras and bangs and taps heard all around the place and seemingly people were starting to enjoy themselves as we entered the bar area and I picked up on a very athletic fit man who told me he was the Social Club pool champion and the landlord realised immediately who it was. He told us the person in question was indeed the pool champion who had passed away suddenly quite recently but he really wanted to know who was smashing beer glasses, turning on the beer pumps and the jukebox along with other misdemeanours. I said to the landlord,

"He says his pool cue is missing and he wants it back"

Landlord's reply," Silly bugger. It's been put up above the bar for safe keeping tell him',

I replied, "He says, no it isn't and that is why he is not in peace right now,

Landlord, "I will get some steps and prove it to him as I can see its case but I can't reach it, if it will make him happy,"

I replied, "He says go on then". The Landlord was not happy about having to go and find some steps as he was quite busy but he mumbled something and disappeared only to reappear with a small set of steps a short while later.

Landlord, "Ask him if I find his cue, will he leave us in peace?"

I replied, "You won't find it", which really infuriated the landlord even more and I could hear him chuntering as he brought the pool cue down in its case and slapped it on the bar. He was covered in dust and a spider scuttled away across the bar, which made some of the party scream possibly for the first time that night.

I said," He says to open it but be careful",

He replied, "Tell him to wait his hurry and will he apologise when I show it to him," but before I could say another word he had opened the case and to his shock and disbelief it was empty.

Landlord, 'I did not know and that is the most amazing piece of spirit evidence I have ever witnessed and as a sceptic I now don't know what to believe". I just grinned and suddenly a ripple of applause rang out around the bar even from my favourite couple who now didn't have any witty quips either. Time to bring them in from the imaginary lamp post in the car park I thought to myself and once again in my time of need spirit had not let me down. The landlord promised to chase up the missing cue if the spirit stopped wrecking the bar on a regular basis but I don't know to this day whether he did or not. Everybody seemed to have had a good night and experienced spirit at work and that there is more to heaven and earth than meets the eye.

It was just before Christmas when Ron rang to ask if we would be up for an investigation at Bosworth Battlefield, which was only a few miles from where we live and has always fascinated me. He had found a window of opportunity as they were holding a Christmas Fayre and so the site would be open until late on that particular night, allowing us to gain access and some nice hot food would help us on our adventure. It was agreed that, weather permitting, the four of us would go ahead with this little adventure deep into the countryside of rural Leicestershire in search of long lost soldiers and what ever else might turn up. I was quite excited by this and couldn't wait for the evening to arrive, but when we got back home, there was a message left on the phone from Lynne, my sister, asking us if we would like to go with them and stay with her daughter Lessa at Valley Farm in Suffolk next to Flatford Mill made famous by the 'The Haywain' - a painting by John Constable a world renowned landscape painter. This day was just getting better by the minute and we knew we would be able to make it as the day in question was Christmas day without even looking at the calendar. Lessa was a teacher at this historical site and was living at Valley Farm at the time, which by the way was an 11th century wattle and daub building which just oozed with history.(Wattle and daub was an ancient building material used for walls involving lattice worked wooden strips daubed with a sticky material such as a mixture of wet clay, soil, sand, animal dung and straw) She was going to be alone there over the Christmas period and had suggested a family gathering and we didn't blame her for that and again the offer was too good to turn down. We more than readily agreed and accepted the invitation, but before that we had to get our minds back on Bosworth Battlefield which was only three days away, so the ghost hunting equipment had to be hurriedly sorted as the Christmas holidays had not yet started.

The evening came around very quickly, or so it felt, as

we headed into the Leicestershire countryside now plunged into darkness as it was around the time of the longest night and soon we would be heading back towards spring that seemed an eternity away. The car park was fairly full as we pulled in for our rendezvous with **Ron and Christine**, the tyres making that familiar sound on deep gravel as I applied the brakes. They were waiting for us and soon we were inside tucking into hog roast rolls with stuffing and apple sauce followed by mince pies and hot mixed spice drinks and, I must say, it was a wonderful way to start a ghost hunt though nobody would have guessed we were on one at that time. Well fed and watered, we made our way back to the cars to put on our warm waterproof coats and hats before grabbing bags of equipment that we would be lumbering around with us all evening. It was a fairly still cold night with not a breath of breeze. A barn owl glided like a silent spectre across the field we were walking down when Ron's K II meter decided to start flashing and I could sense a strong energy surrounding us and a name came into my head which sounded like Latin or Roman and I cannot remember now what it was but why would that happen in a place renowned for a fifteenth century battle I wondered? I was building up the impression of a man on a small stocky looking horse dressed like a Roman soldier, which he had to be from the helmet he was wearing. He was anxious and as soon as we veered from the path he would place his horse in front of us to try to alter our direction as he was protecting something. But what? Ron had been on an organised ghost hunt around the battlefield a few months before and knew everything but as usual he liked to test my abilities to the full (don't you just love brothers) but I must say I did enjoy the challenge and still do. Ron told us where we had been standing was right below a Roman village and this little chap was seen quite frequently in this area, so I was off to a good start then I thought to myself. We said our goodbyes and carried on down the winding path past blackberry bushes now long devoid of fruit and fields with heavy clods of near frozen mud where they had been roughly turned by the plough when we all stopped as we could hear what sounded like volleys of cannon fire in the distance. This occurred twice more in the next half hour and you could see across the vale and there were no fireworks visible and only a handful of smallholdings were dotted about. The ironic thing was that where these sounds where coming from was the same area large amounts of cannon balls were unearthed during an archaeological dig not so long back and we all swore it was cannon fire we heard that night. We were nearing an old railway station but it had nothing to do with what I was sensing now but a feeling of a village with tents, horses, women and children and of course soldiers in uniform which I relayed back to Ron hoping to get a response. He told us that, before the battle, there was an encampment set up in this area and many scenes of this nature had been seen in the area by individuals over the years. It was really dark and creepy as we made our way along the muddy path with sheep in the fields quietly looking up and probably thinking to themselves 'what are those nutters doing out disturbing our peace and quiet', but within seconds Lesley had bellowed in my ear a rendition of what a sheep sounds like and I can't say I didn't nearly jump out of my skin. The K II meter started to flash again randomly now but I was sensing a beggar type person when Lesley stopped and bent down with her torch looking for something. There on the ground was her watch, which she had felt being undone a few minutes earlier and gave good back up evidence as to what I was seeing. Ron could feel someone around his pockets and on a photo taken by Lesley a large orb was seen right in this area and then in a similar position on Christine a few moments later. I tried to tune into this fellow but his accent and dialect was not easy to interpret other than the word "bread" and could this be what he was after I couldn't really tell? He followed us for quite a way, but as we approached a large gnarled oak tree silhouetted spookily against the night sky the roosting wood pigeons and crows took flight issuing distress calls along the way and I could see an archer sitting in it, but the beggar had gone. Christine took a picture and the blue flash blinded us all for a few seconds and then when you looked at the photo a large orb had shown up against the branch I saw him sitting on. Blowing the orb up you could see a man in a tunic and hat with a bow and arrow just like the one I had already made a connection with in my minds eye but he was in hiding so as not to be seen so we moved on once again. We were heading towards the canal when some things occurred that are regularly spoken about in conversation to this day within the family, with some good evidence to back them up, I might add.

We stopped near a notice board with a set of wooden railings behind and open fields across to the canal when Ron began to tell us about an old couple that had had an experience in this area which terrified them and he wondered if I could pick anything up to do with it whatever that was. I was trying to tune into anything or anyone but nothing was coming to me and I thought Ron was going to win this one as we often treated it like a game when I heard horses hooves thundering through the back of my head and then I can't remember much more of the incident but apparently I shouted at the top of my voice,

"Fight with your lives for the honour of your King" and then came the word,

"Charge", long, drawn out and very frightening apparently which I really don't remember saying but when Ron played the EVP back it was there as clear as day and it was pretty scary alright when suddenly Lesley said,

"Look at this" meaning one of the photos she had taken at the time I heard the horses hooves in the back of my head and you could clearly see a thick strip of mist coming from where I was standing that seemed to leap over the wooden fence and across the field. Ironically, the shot taken a few seconds later was completely clear of any mist. Why did the mist seem to leap the fence when normally it would just drift through and that there was none anywhere else we just can't explain? Many have seen this photo and those that have, have no explanations either, so we have to think it was paranormal and if anybody wants to see it I am willing to show it to them.

Nothing much really happened after that except for picking up on two outlaws on the forest path back to the cars who kept their distance thank goodness after telling me that they robbed people but left them in a state where they could not tell tales which was 'dead' and any method went, not people you would want as friends and people were ruthless in those days. It had been a good night and it wasn't even ten o'clock yet and we were on our way home with much to ponder, some good evidence and loads of photos and EVP's to trawl through.

Norma's Monday night circle had moved away from the church now as the large downstairs church was just too big and cold for us in the winter and we had found a college nearer to where all of us lived which was something else strange about our little family as we all lived very close to each other but the six that had dropped out hadn't. I was sad that we were no longer at the church that I loved so much and felt like home, which resulted in me attending more services and seeing some great and truly talented mediums on the rostrum when I was given the chance but it made sense not to have to travel so far on the cold winter nights.

Something strange had happened on the first night at the new venue which I will now relate to you as it was once again very interesting and part of my spiritual development and started shortly after we arrived at the college.

Lesley and I arrived first and having been given directions earlier managed to find our way to the classroom we were hiring for the foreseeable future and as we entered in through the door I instantly did not like it and I walked straight to the far corner of the room and banged shut the cupboard doors that were wide open. There was something in this room and it had come to me for help but I tried to blank it from my mind but that idea turned out to be futile. Everybody had turned up and after a chat and discussing what we had experienced during the week the meditation was about to start. We were going through the colours when I started to see a young girl and then an even younger girl with her and both of them looked very agitated and unhappy and were waving and trying to get my attention but I was still trying to ignore them. Then the nearest computer to us turned itself on and lit up like a Christmas tree and then the banner that was above my head started to swing backwards and forwards very strongly. My meditation was ruined and I prayed that Norma would call the rest of the group back soon but it seemed like an age and then some papers slid off a desk and on to the floor and a tapping started over in the left hand corner of the room. I could have willingly got out of my seat and walked out of the place never to return but I think the two girls would have come home with me but soon the group were back from wherever they had been in their meditation and I thought great I've got nothing to bring to the party which had never happened before. I waited for Norma to speak,

"Pete what do they want, can you ask them", well that was a surprise to me that Norma had sensed them as well so I asked them to step forward and try and show me something I could work with. Firstly I could smell smoke and then I could see flames with the girls trapped behind them but it wasn't a college then but looked more like a farm, which was more than feasible where it was located.

Norma said," Has anybody sent a trapped spirit to the light before", nobody spoke so she continued,

"This will be the exercise for the night, to send these trapped souls to the light and back to their loved ones", this excited me but also any thought that these girls would leave me alone seemed quite appealing right now. Norma took us through the procedure step by step and it was lovely to see the two girls smiling and waving as they passed through the door where rays of really bright light were penetrating through and suddenly all was calm again. The room began to warm up and everywhere seemed brighter and the atmosphere much lighter as we closed the circle for the night having learned a lesson we were not expecting at the start of the evening. We have never had any more problems in that room since but I have always said "Good evening" to the girls ever since on our arrival and "Good night" as we leave. (Not all spirits are trapped souls in my opinion but we all have free will)

Norma became ill for a while after six or seven more meetings but as yet the circle has not reconvened but Norma is much better now and I was once again without a group to further my development in.

Back home, Christmas time was upon us once again and the house was decorated beautifully and the smells of mulled wine and a turkey cooking were in the air but it was Christmas Eve as the next day we would be on our way to Suffolk and Valley Farm which seemed very strange as usually we went nowhere and just chilled. We exchanged presents on Christmas Eve and had a relaxing day, but it still didn't feel right, but we were both excited about where we were going to be staying Christmas night but in hindsight I wish we had stayed at home. We had been weather watching for the last few days praying that snow would not descend upon the land and luckily it hadn't on Christmas day but it was freezing cold with a permafrost and pockets of fog seemed to lurk around every corner as we took a steady drive towards Suffolk with carols playing on the radio and hardly a car on the road - for obvious reasons. It was mid afternoon when we pulled up on the driveway of Valley Farm and what a site we were greeted with as it resembled something out of a Gothic horror film. We were met at the front door with a glass of sherry which lightened the mood a little. It was decorated beautifully and a lot of effort had been put in and dinner smelt lovely especially as we were now so hungry and the fireplace was massive with a huge fire crackling away and when you stood in front of it you could feel your face burning. The place was so old with large areas of stone flooring and staircases that creaked with every movement you made and rooms so big your words would echo around along with your footsteps. It was fascinating but a little scary at the same time, the sort of place that if you wanted to go to the toilet you would wait until somebody else wanted to go for safety in numbers as you felt you were being watched or followed. Dinner was fantastic with that many courses and I lost count of the little extras thrown in along the way but a fun time was had by all as we lounged beside the raging fire while some did their best at charades. Later we sat and told ghost stories, some true especially when it came to my turn when Lessa came in dangling a set of keys and saying,

"Anyone up for a ghost hunt at Flatford Mill and Willy Lott's cottage", I didn't need a second invitation and soon with coats and cameras we were on our way down the lane towards one of the most famous and picturesque buildings in England which we were about to investigate in the dead of a freezing cold night. It was a fantastic old place with an eerie atmosphere, but nothing spectacular was caught over the space of an hour - or so we thought until we were to check the photos taken where a man in a checked shirt could clearly be seen leaning against one of the mill supports. There was nobody of that description in our party and as the place was locked up for the holidays and Lessa had the keys, it had to be spirit. Strangely enough, when we got back home, we downloaded everything from the camera to the laptop, which crashed and everything was lost including that picture and to say we were devastated would have been an understatement. Obviously spirit did not want us to release this picture for some reason but it did not hide our frustrations that such an amazing peace of evidence was now lost for ever.

Back to Valley Farm and it really did look sinister now with the big moon rising above it making the ground glisten in the frost and highlighting the roof to make it look like it had been snowing. I needed a stiff drink once we got back inside and the pull of the large fire was more than appealing as we peeled off our outside clothing. It was nearly one o'clock in the morning when I suggested Lesley and I should go up to bed as it had been a long day and we had to travel back early as my team were playing football later in the day. As we mounted the creaking old rotting wooden staircase I had a feeling sleep would not be on my agenda as we entered the old bedroom with a slanted roof and two single beds so we couldn't even cuddle. It was a long room with a small basin and cupboards at the far end and it wasn't the warmest place in the world with cracks in the window and draughts coming through some of the sills where they had come away from the brickwork and I was really feeling at home - I say in jest. We got into our separate beds after we had pulled them as close together as possible and proceeded to turn the lights off and I put my head under the covers and soon I could hear Lesley snoring away merrily. Great! I thought. The Inn on the Moor all over again which put me on edge but I was so tired I needed my sleep and the harder I tried the worse it got as I tossed and turned in the rickety old bed. Was that a shadow I just saw crossing the wall in front of me? No I thought, more in hope as I pulled the blankets up above my eyes to block my vision from anything that really should not have been there with thoughts that if I let them go they would probably slide down my body to my toes like they did at the Inn on the Moor a few years ago now. The words overactive imagination where pulsating through my brain now and that was how I wanted to keep it until I heard a creak on the floorboard near the door and then heavy footsteps, which definitely didn't belong to Santa Claus, or if they were, he was rather late. They sounded like old fashioned clogs shuffling slowly down the long room but rather loudly in the still of the night and then my bed started to move slowly. At that point I reached for the lamp which wasn't where I had turned it off earlier and finally after much groping I found it having got out of bed and turned the light on, which of course woke Lesley, who was less than amused shall we say, but the only shock I received was that my bed was some ten feet or so from where it had been positioned next to Lesley's when we first came up to bed. Lesley had heard nothing of the footsteps, which wasn't unusual if past experiences were anything to go by and now there was no evidence that anything had been in the room with us at all. We pushed the beds back together and once I had plucked up courage, turned out the lamp that I could now reach easily again so we could get some sleep but that idea was to be short lived as this time within minutes we could both hear the footsteps once again crossing the bedroom and then water running coming from the tap at the far end of the room but neither of us fancied getting out of bed to turn it off as the footsteps were now coming back our way again with the accompaniment of heavy breathing this time, which was an unnecessary accompaniment in my opinion. My bed started to move slowly again, and Lesley informed me in a whisper that hers was doing the same and then the footsteps headed toward the door and disappeared. Eventually I slid out of bed quietly and not without a little trepidation I headed for the sink to turn off the running water while Lesley searched for the lamp, which she eventually found as our beds were the best part of fifteen or so feet from their original positions. Needless to say it was quite a while before either of us went back to sleep waiting for what was coming next but eventually we did and though we heard nothing else I had another experience a while later when a chain of lights appeared in front of the wardrobes and started forming into Yuletide shapes like crackers, bells, and Christmas trees, which I have never got to the bottom of, so was its spirit's way of sending a Christmas message, I would like to think so as I finally drifted off to sleep.

In the morning, when we woke the beds were far apart once again and we were really quite glad to vacate the bedroom from hell once and for all, but downstairs was no better as Lynne and David seemed to be giving us the cold shoulder for some reason. Eventually David said, "What the hell were you lot doing crashing around and walking about all night", as their bedroom was directly below ours and any movement would have been amplified in that old house. I went on to explain what had happened and that we had only got out of bed twice, once to turn the lights on and once to turn the tap off. I don't think they believed us but in that house anything was possible so they let it slide.

The massive fire still had orange glowing embers from the previous night and if you put your hands on the brickwork it was still warm which was nice as the building was cold now being so old and thin walled. Outside was a real Christmas card scene and the really heavy frost looked like snow had fallen and so after a good hearty breakfast we decided to go for a walk before we headed homewards which I wasn't looking forward to due to a lack of sleep.

We unlatched the bolts on the big heavy wooden door and were greeted by a blast of icy cold air and this time it wasn't paranormal just Mother Nature doing her thing. As we walked and talked, our frozen breath could be clearly seen dancing in the stillness of the morning air and a moor hen left a wake as she crossed the river in front of one of Britain's most famous scenes and I thought to myself, how lucky were we to be doing this right now. Through the mist, I could hear mallards calling and wood pigeons cooing, which instantly reminded me of fishing days as a child back at Polstead ponds all those years ago. The watery sun was shining and emitting little or no warmth on this bitterly cold day but to see it highlighting the dew ridden cobwebs hanging from the wooden frame of the mill and surrounding bushes was spectacular and I thanked Spirit for allowing me to be able to witness all this and I felt blessed. We could have spent all day there, cold or not, but soon it was time to go and with a heavy heart realised our adventure was soon to be over. A few weeks before Christmas I would never have dreamed that the holiday period would be spent in one of the most famous country scenes that folk would have on their agenda to visit from all over the world and to prove my point before we left a group, of Japanese tourists had turned up armed with cameras - even in this weather. Back at Valley Farm, Ron and Christine had just turned up as we were saying our goodbyes to everyone as they were staying Boxing Day night (and as I found out later, in our room). We were running late, so any chance of a conversation with them would have to wait for another time as we headed down the long gravel drive with the dark foreboding building now behind us which was where both of us wanted it I think but we nearly didn't get far as a pair of pheasants flew across in front of us and evasive action had to be taken which nearly saw us embedded in a gate post.

It was two days later when Ron rang to tell us about their stay at Valley Farm and some strange occurrences that had happened but before he could say anything else I asked him which room they had stayed in and he told me it was the same one as us. I began to relay to him the events of our night stay and at one point he stopped me and said that they had had the same phenomena involving the footsteps, beds being moved and the tap being turned on and I wasn't surprised in the very least.

Amazing and life saving occurrences

At the Spiritual Church I had got to know many people and there was one particular guy I was being drawn towards, called Rob who ran development circles along with his wife Stacey on a regular basis. He kept saying to me that I should join his group, but I had so many other things going on at the time it just wasn't feasible and transport was difficult with only one car between Lesley and myself.

I was out working one day at a client's I had visited for many years when I noticed by chance a picture of Rob on one of the notice boards and decided to try and find him which I did successfully and we had a good conversation about all things spiritual and every time after that on my visits the same would happen. Each time, he invited me to attend their circle, but it was now about finding the right one that would lead me along the path to where I wanted to go. With more and more ghost hunts and work commitments I once again put it on the back burner, but it would eventually get the better of me.

I was still having strange occurrences in my every day life and I would like to share a few of these with you now as they were amazing.

I will take you back a few years to the time when Lesley and myself started to develop a love for Japanese Koi Carp keeping. We lived in a ground floor flat with a small back garden which was like a jungle with brambles, nettles and dock leaves making it virtually impenetrable and one day in my infinite wisdom I decided to tidy it up. As we started to clear it we began to find things that hadn't seen the light of day for years and at one point we came across an old tin bath, but it was set into the ground as a fishpond that was now home to frogs, toads and other underwater critters. Eventually we had the garden sorted and it looked quite good after all our efforts but what to do with the pond we had unearthed that was our next dilemma. That weekend we found ourselves at the local garden centre looking at goldfish, but we were both being drawn towards some small koi. We went for the pretty ones of course, which was to be a death sentence for them as we really didn't know what we were doing with them other than releasing them into the pond and feeding them. After a constant stream of koi fatalities we had to find out how to keep them safely so a visit to a large garden and aquatics centre was the order of the day and it was while we were there that I noticed a poster on a wall that said,

"Do you fancy spending summer evenings around koi ponds with like minded people and learning all about koi and how to keep them", and it was in Leicester so I hurriedly scribbled down the telephone number on a piece of paper and put it securely in my wallet.

When we got back home from the store in Nottinghamshire, which was even stranger as this group was in Leicester, I fetched the number from my wallet and rang it. A well spoken man answered the phone and gave me directions on how to get to his place for the meeting on that coming Tuesday night after telling us that we were more than welcome to come along. We really didn't know what to expect that evening when we knocked on his door and were ushered round the side and into his back garden which was immense and as we followed the path we came across his raised pool of crystal clear water with koi of all shapes and sizes gracefully swimming about in a seemingly effortless motion. We had not expected anything like this and were bitten by the bug straight away and a bigger pond was to be our first project as soon as we could find the time. We met some lovely people that night all with an interest in koi but one person Lesley already knew and he was Dave, one of her tutors during her University degree course. She introduced me to him and very soon we were good friends, especially after he had taught me to fly fish. He was a brilliant fly fisherman and could have fished for his country, but was to be taken from this earthly plane far too early for anybody's liking. Dave was a guy who could turn his hand to anything and his love for koi was infectious and anybody he got to know, ended up keeping them. One day, he invited us to meet another of his friends who was a real koi enthusiast with fish from Japan that won shows all over the country. Lesley and I hit it off straight away with him and his family and over a few years we all became close friends and our lives revolved around koi and anything associated with them. We built a thousand gallon koi pool at the back of the flat with filters and everything needed to keep koi healthy and happy and so were we. It was at one of my friends special occasions that Dave dropped the bombshell that his cancer had returned and it was now untreatable which took the wind out of everybody's sails as how could such a lovely guy be made to suffer like this? Dave had just moved to a house in the country where he had built an eight thousand gallon koi pool in a garage and it was awesome along with anything else that he put his hands to. My friend had been made redundant and had managed to get a job with the same company that I now worked for so he was in a good place right now, but Dave's news had knocked the stuffing out of him. Dave's health deteriorated very quickly and soon he was gone to the spirit side of life where I hope he is fly fishing, entertaining folk and keeping koi. The day of his funeral came and the weather was atrocious with gale force winds and driving rain soaking everyone from head to foot, which knowing Dave he had organised from somewhere in the spirit realms and as I said he could turn his hand to anything. Myself and Dennis from our village, who I mentioned earlier, decided to honour Dave by going in full fly fishing gear including, waders, waistcoats and floppy hats adorned with trout and salmon flies and we hoped he liked it and could think of no better way to send him off. The day had only one real issue and that was the fact that Dave's headstone was not ready in time and though every effort was made to sort the issue out it didn't happen which was very stressful for the family. A year later it wasn't sorted and we all really thought it would never happen but when it did it was amazing. Dave's wife and children had moved away from the area to start a new life which Dave had suggested when he came through at a reading where he also said she was about to meet a new partner and it was with his blessing and this happened within a matter of weeks . The grave wasn't really being attended to, and was still minus a headstone. My friend and Dave's best friend were visiting a company client one day in the village where Dave had lived and he had rang me to tell me so and I suggested he pay Dave's grave a visit and say hello from the both of us. He then said he had been thinking about that and that was one of the reasons he had rang me. It was only half an hour later when he rang me back sounding very shaky and quite tearful and he went on to tell me that when he had gone round the back of the church and along the path towards Dave's grave he found two men with a mini digger, lowering his headstone onto his grave and it was in place as he reached his plot. They say timing is everything and this was to the split second, perfect. Probably two and a half years after his passing and his best friend was there to share it with him and all he could say was,

"How about that for a coincidence", I could have throttled him, willingly at that exact moment.

My reply " Wake up and smell the coffee mate, Dave got you here to see this and isn't spirit just wonderful?", He was the biggest sceptic I have ever met and I thought I was bad in the past, but this was all about to change in this next situation.

We step forward a few years now, to more recent times and my friend's world was being turned upside down with his marriage over and on the verge of losing his job which was so sad because everything had been going so well for him but suddenly changes were a foot. I had known about his situation for a while but had kept a safe distance hoping he could sort it out but that didn't seem to be the case and he was shutting himself off from the world or so it seemed. It was one Friday lunchtime when my phone rang and it was my friend who seemed very distressed telling me he had taken half a day off and said he was going home as his mind was all over the place, then he said,

"Thanks for being a good mate and I will see you one day", that had the alarm bells ringing and I immediately rang my boss and told him the situation and I suggested I go round and see him and to my surprise my boss agreed. I was about forty miles away so I wasn't just round the corner, but distance is not a factor when someone is in trouble and my subconscious was telling me that was the case. Eventually I turned down his road where his van was parked but I stopped a distance away so as to surprise him when I knocked the door and it worked when my very shocked friend opened the door to see me standing there. He was speechless and he looked very haggard and dishevelled at that precise moment but he had to invite me in as he had no real option other than to slam the door in my face and I was now already inside. He seemed quite calm but I think he was planning a way to get rid of me, as on the table was a bottle of spirit, no longer full by any means, and a pack of rather strange looking objects which turned out to be ampules of morphine. He was intending to take his life and it didn't look like anything was going to stop him as it seemed to have been planned meticulously. How could I stop him? I started rambling on about anything to turn his attention away from what he was doing but I needn't have worried as spirit were about to step in to save the day. He made us both a cup of coffee and I asked him,

"What the hell are you thinking of? There must be an alternative solution?" but his only reply was,

"Why not?", and this wasn't getting us anywhere so I needed another plan quickly but before I could say anything for some reason he stood up and headed to his computer and said,

"Look at these koi I have ordered from Japan, what do you think", and as with any of his koi they were stunning,

"Beautiful" I said, then out of the blue, he went on,

"Did I show you the pictures from the Halloween party fancy dress I went to where I won first prize", which seemed a bit strange but I went with it while he scrolled through. Some of the costumes where pretty awesome, I must admit, but his dressed as the Grim Reaper was by far and away the best and I think if you had seen him on the street you would have died from shock. As I looked at his picture, which was full length, I noticed a large bright orb below the knee and I was being drawn towards it as there was something inside it I needed to investigate. I asked him if he could blow it up but his computer did not have that facility so I got him to email it to me so I could investigate it when I finally returned home. He said that he had never noticed that orb before but even he could see that it was as clear as the nose on your face and that there was something in it. I began to sense that his Mum from spirit side had now entered into the conversation and as he would listen and do anything for her I told him so and I guessed she was responsible for the orb. I had made communication a few times previously with her to help him through difficult situations but he never believed it was really her but I knew she was worried for her son and was trying to stop him from doing something stupid. The rest of the afternoon went rather better and it was too late to go back to work but that didn't bother me particularly as I had my friend's welfare to think about. It was nearly six o'clock in the evening when I left his house after asking him for assurances that he would not do anything stupid once I had gone, but I only had his word for that. I arrived home and got straight onto the laptop to find the emailed picture he had sent and soon I had it on the screen and proceeded to blow it up and what I found was amazing. There in front of me was the cartoon face of Tigger and below it was an object that looked like a stick which I asked Lesley to look at as well and she referred to it as an ampule and then it clicked, it was an ampule of morphine, a message sent in an orb from his mother in spirit. His

Mum's name was Whinnie and as a couple, their nicknames were Pooh and Tigger, so there was the link. I was shocked by this and returned an email to my friend with the blown up orb and a description of what I had found stating that this was his Mum's way of telling him it is not his time and a whole new chapter in his life awaited him. I received no reply and two hours later I tried to ring him but still there was no reply. I can't say I wasn't worried that he may have done something stupid after I left, but I trusted in spirit that they knew what they were doing. I had a bad nights sleep tossing, turning and worrying, but I couldn't sense that anything untoward had happened. I rang again at eight o'clock the next morning and still no reply, so I needed to get over there as soon as possible to see what was going on but I had things to do first and just as I was about to leave I tried to ring once more and to my blessed relief he answered. He had drank a lot which finally got the better of him and he had fallen asleep at the table and now was left with a banging headache but he was still with us and that was what mattered right now. He had received the email and could not believe his eyes when he opened it and realising it was from his Mum, spirit side, he had cried out for help and put the ampules back in the cupboard. He then went on to say,

"Its not very often that I am shocked and speechless but this is one of those times as I have no answer for what has just happened and I now believe you can communicate with spirit and I am sorry for doubting you even though previous events had made me think and I promise I will not do anything stupid again". I was greatly relieved by this and my belief in spirit and what they are capable of was once again enhanced in the most unusual way and possibly a life was saved at the same time.

It was later the next week I was talking to him on the phone from my van when I felt his Mum's energies around me who had a message for her son, which I relayed to him,

" Tell him all will be well and in a short space of time

he will be living in a foreign country and he will realise why I had to step in and stop him from doing something stupid as he has a life to lead". It was later that week his contract was terminated with the company he worked for and he was in great danger of losing his house and I just hoped he would not return to his dark thoughts. We seemed to lose contact after that for a period of time as he never seemed to answer his phone to me but six months or so later I found out that he had met another lady and was now living on another continent as his Mum in spirit had predicted.

I feel that orb on his fancy dress costume was meant for me to see and that spirit can manipulate anything as and when they need to but what really shocked me was the ability of spirit to send messages in an orb, which is truly remarkable.

My Abilities are tested

Spring was just around the corner and the caravan season was looming closer, which always brought added excitement into our lives after a long cold winter but our first commitment when we made it to Wales this year was the scattering of Samba's ashes 'The Loveable Rogue' and a good send off was needed for the old boy. There was nowhere better than his favourite river Tiefi above the salmon pools where he played and swam for many years, whatever the weather and condition of the river, which was a large powerful salmon river. With so many memories, it had to be here and so it was agreed that that would be his final resting place and a Welsh friend of ours who he knew well would join us on the day to pay her respects. The day came and it was sunny but cold as spring usually is and the river was nearly full but still below its banks so we could follow the path along as far as possible so the ashes could journey downstream to his favourite pool above the rapids. All three of us eventually reached the place where we were going to release the ashes into the river, and we said a little prayer and our goodbyes before tipping the ashes into the chocolate brown raging torrent and watching them disappear. We must have stood in that spot reminiscing for ten minutes or more before our friend threw a daffodil into the water out of respect. To our disappointment, it got firmly wedged under some tree branches, which was a shame as we wanted it to travel down the length of the river to his pool, but that now wasn't going to happen. We all made our way back to his pool further down and to our amazement, there was the daffodil in the middle of his pool and it hadn't passed us and as far as we were concerned it was thoroughly stuck back up the river. We took this to be a sign that the old boy was ok and happy where we had left him as we made our way over the long stone bridge and headed towards the local pub for a nice hot pub lunch.

Across the road was a restaurant and downstairs was a little Aladdin's Cave full of all things spiritual, from crystals and incense burners to tarot cards and as I am always drawn to these places I had to take a look again. I loved this place and the energies were so strong I never wanted to leave and today was no different. I had tried tarot cards and never felt comfortable with them but there was one particular pack that I was being drawn to and they where Native American Animal Medicine cards which with my Spirit Guide was not surprising. Lesley could see I really liked them and to cheer me up bought a pack, which I still use to this day. We left the cellar and reemerged into bright sunlight that hurt your eyes after the darkness and made our way back over the bridge, which Samba would have passed under on his final journey to the sea, and back to the car park. It had been a lovely morning and a grand send off for Samba, but now it was back to the caravan to start our holiday and have a look at my newly purchased cards though I thought the end result would probably be the same as my previous tarot experiences but how wrong was I again.

Near the caravan was a lane, with a deep glen on one side with a babbling brook running along the bottom which Lesley was not over keen on especially when dusk fell and never in the dark and she had asked on previous occasions could I sense anything. I had picked up on a very agitated man who was looking for his daughter and I left it at that. I had been fishing off the beach one day and on the way back along the lane I could sense someone behind me and when I turned I saw a young girl and she was soaked from head to foot and I gathered she must have drowned and many years ago by the clothes she was wearing. I asked her where she had drowned and she told me in the lake but there was no lake I was aware of in the area and when I looked again she had gone leaving me with a mystery I needed to solve. A few days later, I was talking to one of the neighbours near the site and asked him if he knew of a girl that had drowned in the area and surprisingly he knew of an incident many years ago that was written about in a book where a young girl had drowned in the lake. Which lake, I asked him, and told me that the caravan site and his extensive garden where once all part of a deep lake and this shocked me.

Lesley had gone back home and left me at the van for a week or so with one of our Labradors and on walking back up the lane one evening from a lovely trek along the beach, I sensed the young girl again who this time skipped along beside me quite excitedly and I thought to myself should I try and send her to the light now that I had the experience of how to do it. I asked her if she would like to see her family again as I began to visualise a door with a light penetrating through it from the other side as before. She smiled and walked slowly towards the door when suddenly a man grabbed her hand which worried me a little until they both turned round to wave and I realised it was the girls father and they were back together once again as they passed through the open door into the arms of waiting loved ones. Since then we have never experienced any negative energy along the lane at dusk but it still remains creepy in the dead of night, unsurprisingly.

Soon it was time to leave Wales after a great holiday and return home and before we knew it we were back on the sofa in our little village which was always a bit of a downer as there was tons of mail to sort through and answerphone messages to pick up and there was only one from Ron. It turned out something was going on at their house with strange occurrences happening on a far too regular basis for his and Christine's liking. Objects had been visibly moving and footsteps clearly heard on the stairs along with the intruder alarm going off and the doorbell ringing when nobody was there. They wondered if I would take a look to help ease their minds and as I was not due back at work for a few more days sooner than later would be good. I rang back and they sounded very agitated and it was agreed that Lesley and myself would go and see them the following morning and not to worry as there had to be a reason why this activity was happening. It was about ten o'clock the next morning when we pulled up on their driveway and everything looked quite calm and peaceful until Ron appeared with a worried look on his face which wasn't his usual greeting I must say. He ushered us into the house and almost immediately I felt an uneasy atmosphere as I went to sit down. As I looked round on the side was a model hot air balloon that rocked in its mounting which was the way it was designed and it was now rocking in front of my eyes and I nudged Lesley to point it out to her but she had already seen it. I could feel a cold chill down one side and realised spirit was trying to communicate with me, but who could it be? I soon recognised that the person communicating was Christine's Mum and she was upset and began to tell me that her husband had been trying to make contact with the family as he had seen the error of his ways and learnt his lessons from when he had been in the physical world but when I told Ron and Christine this all they could say was,

"What does he expect" but the rest is very personal to them so I shall not go into any details. It was Christine's Mum who was moving the objects about and making the bells ring as she was fed up with hearing conversations about all the bad things he had done and it was time to put an end to it. I relayed her message once again and this time it seemed to strike a chord and after a short conversation between themselves they offered to hold out the olive branch, as the saying goes, if the activity stopped and things went back to normal. Almost immediately the room seemed to become brighter and warm up which was quite nice as outside it was cold. They had offered a kind of apology to Christine's Dad though there was still no love lost between them I felt. I suddenly began to see what looked like a double decker open topped bus with Christine's family on board and this had been sent directly from her Father as a memory link that he wanted to share and she recognised it immediately which made her smile. Things seemed to have calmed right down and Ron and

Christine offered to visit her parent's grave to pay their respects and place some flowers, which seemed to appease them and the rest of the visit passed without any further incidents. After another cup of coffee it was time to return home and sort out everything that had just been left where we dumped it when we got home from Wales the night before and tomorrow we would be back to work, which wasn't the nicest thought in the world.

Back at work things were going along nicely now and then out of the blue spirit grabbed me again when I was least expecting it. One of my clients was an Asian dentist's and I had always got on well with the owners and on this particular day I had just finished my routine checks and I was writing my report while drinking a very welcome cup of coffee when I threw my pen down as I could see a man and it looked like he was feeding monkeys or working with them at least and I felt he belonged to the lady on the reception desk. I asked her if she knew of anybody in spirit who would have kept monkeys but she could shed no light on this so I explained what I was seeing and then she remembered that her uncle had lived close to a temple in India where he had fed the monkeys daily for many years but he had passed away at too early an age. I started to speak in an Asian tongue and came out with a name, which apparently was the name of her uncle which was very strange as I don't speak anything but English and a smattering of French. Then I saw him waving a yellow chrysanthemum at her and I told her that he said she would recognise the significance of this and well she nearly fell through the floor and so did I when she told me about it. It was a case that herself and two sisters were not allowed to attend his funeral which greatly upset them so when it was quiet they each stole a flower from one of the garlands that draped his coffin and hid them, pressing them in between the pages of a book where they remain to this day and nobody could know this so she was amazed. Her family asked me if I would do a group reading for them one evening but as of yet I have not followed up their request but maybe one day when I get around to it as they are such lovely people.

Another incident within the Asian community occurred one afternoon at a restaurant in town when I was working once again but the circumstances were different this time. I had been visiting this site for a number of years and I had got to know the family and the owner and they never let me leave without something to eat and drink but today as I walked through the door all I could see were sad faces and the place seemed lifeless but they were still open. One of the family took me to one side and told me that the owner had passed away suddenly and it was not a good time for any of them but the business was not in any danger as it was family run. It was coming up to Diwali (The festival of light) but they were not looking forward to the celebrations in any form and it had hit them hard but as I sat there drinking my drink I sensed the owner's presence sitting opposite me who told me to tell them,

"To get off their backsides and cheer up as he was fed up with them moping around scaring off customers and that they were to enjoy Diwali in his memory", I passed the message on and it went down like a lead balloon and as usual I said,

"Don't shoot the messenger," and I left after getting my paperwork signed. It was six weeks later when I returned to the restaurant that I got a real surprise when one of the family said,

"Have you got any more messages for us please", apparently they had taken on board what I had said and had enjoyed the Diwali celebrations more than ever before and had felt the owner's spirit with them all night. I felt my hair being tickled and I knew who that was and I just looked at them with a broad smile on my face and carried on with my work as usual.

It was a few weeks later when I was asked to work for a couple of days in Norfolk and I would have to stay over in a motel so arrangements were made for this to happen and I really needed the rest as the work I was doing was physical and demanding so I was glad to get back to the motel for something to eat and drink after a long refreshing shower. When it came to bedtime I put out the lights and turned the TV off and lay on the bed to let the aches and pains of the day fade away but light was coming through the window from a treatment plant across the way slightly illuminating the room. It was then I noticed a ladies hairbrush on the long desk across the room which started to move and vibrate but as I was so tired I dozed off and thought nothing more about it. At one point during the night, I was awoken feeling really cold and on the bedside table was a picture portrait of a young girl but again I fell back to sleep again. When I awoke in the morning it suddenly dawned on me what I had experienced during the night was very strange and no there was no ladies hairbrush on the desk and the portrait of the young girl was only a notice regarding breakfast choices so I don't know what to make of it to this day. I was glad it was only a one night stop over but its in the book as I found it highly interesting and I hope you did as well. Could she have come with a warning as I started to suffer dizzy spells the next day and I had to go on the sick. I drove back home slowly wondering if I would ever see my wife and Labradors again? I did but I was sick for a long period of time. You never know what you're going to get when you stay in strange places for a night and this is one of the reasons why ghost hunting fascinates me now and always will.

    Lesley and myself tried a few organised ghost hunts for a while and though they were interesting there is nothing like running your own as we had in the past but a group was to come to me sooner than I realised and it was everything I wanted.

The right groups

It was once again through work that I got severely bitten by the ghost hunting bug again but thinking back was it fate as it ticked every box for me.

I had been visiting a school on a routine basis for a number of years and I had got to know the maintenance man quite well over this period of time and on one occasion towards the end of the days work he took me on a little guided tour of the old place. As I walked round a corner to a large staircase I noticed a man laying on the stairs and it felt as if he had experienced a heart attack and passed immediately and this was later verified and other little things occurred during our walk round so I asked what the possibility of doing a ghost hunt there would be. He said it shouldn't be a problem but he would have to discuss it with the school and, unsurprisingly, I heard no more.

It was quite a while before I visited again due to other work commitments but when I did I got quite a surprise as the maintenance guy told me there was to be an organised ghost hunt in the near future by an experienced group and I could join them if I wanted too. This was an absolute must for me and he gave me the number of the person running it, who was called John and said,

"Have a chat with him, as you seem to be singing off the same hymn sheet so you can share your ideas". By this time I had built up a lot of my own equipment and it really wasn't doing much besides gathering cobwebs and dust so I needed to ask John if I could bring my own stuff on his investigation and treading on toes came to mind. Next day I rang him but got no reply which was a little disappointing as I had built myself up with all the questions and answers in my head that I thought I would need but finally when I did get through I was in for a shock. John was as enthusiastic as I was about all things paranormal and our initial phone conversation lasted for three quarters of an hour and we each had so much input during the conversation neither of us wanted to put the phone down. The two weeks until the investigation flew by and John had asked me to be there early so we could get set up and I could bring any equipment I wanted to use, so to say I was excited was an understatement. I knew the size of the building and it wasn't small so it would have to be well covered and would our equipment do it I wasn't sure until I realised there were more than just us two of us with equipment setting up. The hunt was for charity and guests were to arrive later to allow us time to have cameras in the cellars, on the stairs and in other reputedly haunted areas and it really began to feel like a professional ghost hunt. The night was a quiet one, as most are in truth, but the chance to work along side such dedicated ghost hunters was an absolute joy and we had a lot of fun along the way. We were packing away about four o'clock in the morning, when John invited me on their next hunt and I couldn't believe my luck to be invited to work with this team once again and it was to be at another school in the not to distant future. As we left, he thanked me for my help and making the evening go without a hitch and I returned the compliment to him and the others.

It wasn't long before we were off again and I had purchased some new bits of equipment as you do with the highlight being 'Tigger' a stuffed tiger that would light up and sound an alarm if touched or approached. Again it was to be an all night vigil and all in aid of charity so plenty of coffee and food to keep us awake was the order of the night. This school had a totally different feel from the moment we walked into the place and I had a feeling something might just happen and there weren't many of us so we could all stay together, safety in numbers and all that. Some of the corridors seemed to run for miles into far distant rooms that had a sinister feeling about them that I was picking up on and everything about the place made me feel uneasy. You get those kind of nights every so often but I was surprised when John threw me a walkie-talkie so I could lead a group and that made me feel very important and definitely part of the team now. One of the regulars called Jane, and myself, decided to go for a walk around the building before the main investigation started and in hindsight was not the cleverest idea as walking along one corridor we heard three loud bangs and when I repeated the noise it happened again and was followed by a real guttural laugh which made us leave that particular area rather more quickly than we had both expected back to the others and the safe area. This was not the first time strange occurrences had happened when we had gone off alone and eventually we were to be used as bait in cellars and such like as we seemed to attract things lets put it like that. It was at one point we were all in a long corridor when the lights went out and the doors started to bang and 'Tigger', who I mentioned earlier, started to go crazy with lights flashing and emitting an ear piercing alarm as panic set in among us as we couldn't get out of the corridor and it felt like we were the hunted not the hunters. Eventually things seemed to calm and we managed to open the doors and get back to the safe room for a well earned cup of coffee and a calm down after experiencing something we had no answers for. Throughout the night, we were hearing footsteps and strange noises and whenever we went upstairs to investigate an area the downstairs security lights would come on and visa versa. It was a night I will never forget, and I shared it with like minded people who were professional in their attitude and great fun to be with and it was wonderful to be back doing regular ghost hunts again.

I bumped into Rob again at his place of work and we had our usual conversation and as I had nothing planned for the following Sunday I said I would pay a visit to his and Stacey's circle at the church and I was true to my word. I turned up and I didn't know anyone in the circle other than the tutors but by the end of the session I was friends with everyone especially two up and coming mediums called Sara and Michelle and I couldn't wait to go again. I had never done platform readings as such before and after going on the rostrum and realising you are surrounded by spirit I felt right at home and I gave two lovely messages and I was now realising I had found the group I was meant to be in for so long. After a few weeks it began to feel that I was becoming part of a spiritual family and mixing with some very good mediums. I soon had Rob and Stacey on social network along with various members of the group but something had to change and it wasn't long before a bombshell was dropped on me in the form of redundancy on health grounds which I had no idea was coming.

A few days later after the news had spread Norma rang out of the blue to see if I was ok and to ask me a question,

"Hey Pete, when are you going to write a book about your ghost hunting adventures and spiritual development as it would be fascinating and now you have the time",

I replied, "Norma what a great idea, I'm going to start it now," and that is exactly what I have done. After we had finished our phone conversation I went a found a pen and pad and started to write a template for the new book and I felt a twinge of excitement ripple through my body and I knew this was meant to happen.

I was to spend the next couple of months up in Wales at the caravan writing and once again I was in a good place and it felt as if the book was writing itself as large portions of my day where spent writing but I still needed some time for myself, so I would take the dog with me and walk into New Quay and sit on the harbour wall in the warm sun and soak in the views that I used to recharge my batteries which were enhanced whenever the local pod of bottle nosed dolphins made an appearance. I was on the way back one sunny afternoon without a care in the world when I tripped on a rock and fell down smashing my phone in my pocket and people came running from everywhere as what they had seen was a really heavy fall and thought I might be badly injured but except for a few cuts and bruises I was fine which was surprising as I had fallen heavily on rocks. Strangely enough, it felt like someone, probably one of my guides had cushioned my fall probably because they were keen on finishing my book as soon as possible. I dusted myself down and as I hobbled along the coast path I passed a family that had a little jack russell running along with them but as I got closer to them they had no dog and no one was carrying a lead either so my spiritual abilities weren't damaged in any way but I didn't say anything to the family as I didn't want to push my luck anymore that day.

Finally, the day came that the book was to be finished and there was one small section about Dunkirk still to be finished and as Lynne knew where we had been as I really couldn't remember enough of the episode I put it on the back burner until she rang me back which she did later in the day. As we were talking little black asterix started to appear where once were words and before I knew it the book was encrypting itself for no apparent reason and I was devastated and as only the first sixty pages were backed up I was in real trouble and feared the worst. It turned out, over forty seven thousand words were lost and I felt like giving the book up but I knew spirit wanted my story out there so I recovered what I could and started again and hopefully this time you will get to read it.

Of course, while I was away, circle was on hold for me and I am now busily playing catch up as I head towards my goal of becoming a platform medium and feel right back at home in my group. All mine and spirits hard work is paying off as since I thought I had finished the book things have further developed for me. My messages have started to get stronger and my confidence is growing by the day and circles are now becoming part of my everyday life. It was after one of these sessions that Rob and Stacey invited Inga (another up and coming platform medium) and myself to work along side them at a Coping with Cancer charity event that weekend and as nothing was standing in the way we both agreed to do it. We were being let loose on the general public so we felt we must have attained a certain level of credibility to be offered such a massive leap from circle.

The day came and the clock seemed to whizz round to the time when my tutors would pick me up on the beginning of a new adventure. I cannot say that I wasn't having second thoughts as we walked into the hall with tables and chairs laid out in front of us but I trusted in spirit that they would work with me and as it turned out they did. Stacey and Rob each had a leather bag with them one depicting a Native American Indian scene and a dream catcher which belonged to Stacey and I really liked it but I wondered what it contained as I had never attended anything like this before. As she started to decant this cavernous bag out came a beautifully ornate tablecloth followed by angel statues and candleholders and Rob did much the same on his table transforming the place into what I can only describe as a spiritual bazaar. Two o'clock soon came around and the public were queuing for their chance of a mini reading and I felt a pit in my stomach as the first lady approached us but this was what I had wanted for the last ten years or so and I had been given the opportunity at last. Inga was sitting with Rob and I was sitting with Stacey at separate tables and within what seemed only a matter of seconds Stacey was telling the lady in front of us all about how she was feeling and what was going on in her life right now and I was left in awe as the lady began sobbing at the accuracy of the message but where could I interject in all this.? All of a sudden I was visualising an older lady standing to her right I felt was her grandma and she verified this when I told her. The message I gave was profound and, to tell you the truth, I was starting to enjoy myself as more validation poured through from the spirit world. Soon that ladies time was up and she was replaced by a man and then another woman, a youngish girl and so on and so on, each one having a spirit around them I could see through my third eye with strong messages for all of them. I always felt I was playing catch up with Stacey who flew out of the blocks every time without fail and it was amazing but she said the same about me without the flying out the blocks bit as I certainly didn't. Inga was doing really well with Rob and she soon had a lady crying but they were tears of joy and validation which it is what it is all about really as their loved ones speak. I was really enjoying the afternoon now and my nerves had subsided substantially and I think Inga's had as well when Stacey turned to me and said,

"You're doing great Pete, what are you doing Monday evening as we have a psychic supper over in Coventry and I would like you to work with me again," and before I had time to think my mouth had replied,

"Ok let's give it go".

My mouth has got me into a lot of trouble over the years but this time it felt right and I found myself relishing the opportunity of reading for the public again. The afternoon was finally over and both Inga and myself felt exhausted, probably from the amount of spiritual energy we had used up in such a short space of time, at least that's what it felt like even though it was three hours. Everything was packed away and a decent amount of money had been raised for Coping with Cancer and that made me feel good as I was dropped off back at home thinking over what had just occurred and did I really see those peoples relatives and friends in spirit. We are taught to TRUST in everything spirit shows and tells you but I still always find myself doubting my abilities and I require a good swift kick up the backside at times.

The next day was our lovely Sunday circle and much of the talk was about how well Inga and myself had performed on the Saturday which was a little embarrassing, as I now had to recreate that standard during circle once again. It wasn't long before I was bringing through solid messages once again from the spirit world and feeling in my element that brings me so much joy these days. Everybody did really well as usual and the energies were good and strong with laughter and tears along the way as you see everybody works in their own unique way. Nobody is better than anyone else only some are more experienced than others. Once circle had finished I stayed behind and we discussed about the following day and the psychic supper in Coventry my big mouth had led me into.

I would pick Rob and Stacey up this time as we had to be there for six o'clock in the evening and the venue was closer to them than myself but nothing could have prepared me for the evenings events that where to unfold at a psychic supper. I had never been to one of these events before, not even as a customer so I really didn't know what to expect right now. I found myself clock watching through the day as a condemned man probably would have before his last rites were read but for some reason I really was excited deep down underneath. I left in plenty of time to pick the others up and everything was on schedule as I arrived at their house and with only twenty five miles to travel in just over an hour I could see no real issues occurring. Unfortunately there had been an accident on the M6 and though we weren't using the motorway the diverted traffic was going to have a major part to play in our slow progress to the Spiritualist Church. The roads were solid and time was now our worst enemy as we crawled painfully slowly towards our destination. It was three minutes to six as we pulled up and with the event starting at six o'clock things were tight. Craig, the organiser, was standing outside on the road as we had driven past and must have breathed a sigh of relief when he saw us. We had to park a distance away so a gentle jog was required to meet our deadline and momentarily my mind was taken away from the impending situation I was about to face. As we walked through the church doors I could hear the noise of expectant folk eagerly a waiting a good evening being linked with the spirit world and to my horror the place was packed. Daniel and the lion's den instantly came to mind, but I was to be proved oh so wrong as spirit will never let you down. There were eight long tables with eight people around each of them and a spare chair at the end for the medium making a total of sixty four members of the public if my maths serves me correctly. I suddenly felt rather isolated as we were ushered into the back like teachers into their staff room. Now I was sitting amongst other well known mediums and I thought to myself, how have I come this far in such a small space of time and the answer is quite simple really, through spirit. A quick glass of water for Dutch courage and to help open up the lines of communication with spirit and I could hear prayers and blessings being said and then the dreaded bell rang which was what it felt like at this particular moment trust me. I was to work with Stacey again and bring in my two penneth as and when, as I thought to myself fat chance of that. The object is to give as many messages on a table inside twenty minutes before the bell rang again and you moved to another and anyone whom had not received a reading first time around where your priority. This would happen three times over the course of the evening and we were suddenly underway and Stacey was off like the proverbial racehorse with her messages but I wasn't far behind. At first things were a little slow but as the energies started to flow, spirit were everywhere and people once again could take who I was seeing and speaking with from the spirit world and at times Stacey and I found ourselves double linking with the same spirit and that was awesome. It didn't seem five minutes since we started and the bell had already sounded again for us to move and I was really starting to enjoy this event now. I knew spirit would not let me down and the validations were accepted eagerly by the recipients and the energies were so high now I felt like I was walking through clouds something I had never experienced before. When the final bell went I hoped we would be doing another table, but sadly that was not the case. I had survived what had turned out to be the greatest night of my spiritual journey so far and Stacey turned and smiled and I knew I had done ok and as all the mediums retreated to the staff room there was a table laid out with food upon it for us to eat and I felt at peace with the world. I had to pinch myself sitting there with other gifted mediums and I thought to myself, my time has finally arrived - thank you spirit. I was on a high for days after, and to tell you the truth, I can't really remember the drive home from Coventry but don't tell Rob and Stacey (that's our little secret) or they probably would freak at the thought. After the evenings events I was introduced to some of the churches staff and one medium turned to Rob and said,

"He's going to make a great medium" and I can't tell you what that did for my belief and trust in spirit.

It was a few days later while minding my own business that an email came through from the spiritualist church in Coventry asking me if I would be prepared to carry out a clairvoyant service for them and I just looked at it in complete and utter shock thinking they had sent it to the wrong person, but they hadn't. I have never done a platform rostrum service before even with another person so I rang Stacey who always tells it like it is,

"Just say you will do it Pete," I thought it's alright for you you've been there, done it and got the t-shirt while I'm still shopping. She suggested that she would do a service with me if that helped which did put my mind at rest but I didn't reply to the churches email straight away. Finally I did, saying that I was honoured to be asked and that as I had never taken a clairvoyant service before Stacey had offered to take one with me or words to that effect and I thought to myself why me and why now.

It was later that evening that the reply came back from Jon who had sent the original communication saying,

"I understand that you are nervous but feed off this energy and I would be prepared to share the rostrum with you if needs be but you should trust in your own abilities. My wife was on one of the tables and the feedback from her and her friends was so positive and your messages so strong we would love to see you work here," I nearly dropped through the floor when I read the reply and I thought, me a platform medium and its going to happen rather more quickly than I had ever anticipated. Thank you Rob and Stacey and all those who have helped me along the way so far you know who you are and those that shot me down in flames as you have only made me stronger and I look forward to the next episode on my spiritual journey which seems to alter on a near daily basis now. Saying that, since my book was sent for proof reading I have done church services, private house and group readings and my diary is filling up for next year and I feel serving spirit is now becoming my life.

Since then I have found out that Rob and Stacey and some of the others are into ghost hunting and have since become a part of our group and I hope to share many more investigations with them so I can tell you of our findings as my amazing life continues. I would not have changed any of it if I had the chance again and I hope this autobiography has answered some questions about things you may have experienced and not understood and if you are on your spiritual journey enjoy it and I hope its as good as mine so until the next volume hits the shelves I wish you all good health, wealth and happiness on your life journey but It doesn't end there as the most amazing revelation has just occurred that I cannot leave out and I would like to share with you now.

I have been sitting in Rob and Stacey's circle for six months or more now and around the same time one person had joined our circle and his name is Peter.

All of us brought through beautiful messages for loved ones week after week and still do. If you have ever sat in a circle you will know the energies but on one occasion I brought Peter's brother through with a message which was well received but I did not realise the impact this particular message would have only a few weeks later.

Thoughts of Caroline Clare had been coming into my head for some reason and I wondered where and how she was as the last time I saw her she was very poorly a few years previous. We had decided to try and find her but every avenue on the Internet lead us down a blind alley. It was very strange that nobody had contacted us so we did not know what had happened and as you know Caroline would always test me too the limit.

Lesley had a dental appointment and decided to drop me off with the Labradors at the arboretum where mum and dads tree is. She would pick me up later and I liked that idea.

It was a real autumn morning with golden leaves spiralling and tumbling to the floor in the strong breeze and the bottom of my trousers were sodden from the heavy dew overnight in the long meadow grass. The dogs were straining at the leash as squirrels collecting acorns scampered up the nearest trees to evade the unwanted attention of the Labradors. The church bells were ringing in the nearby church where parent's funeral's had both been carried out not so many years ago. Eventually we found our way to their tree, which by the way was still full of greenery while every other round and about had turned gold and were rapidly loosing their leaves. I had my usual chat with them but on this occasion I asked if they could help me find Caroline Clare and it was eating away at me. This was on the Thursday before the revelations occurred the very next week. I went to the following Sunday and Wednesday night circles but the one on the Thursday will stay with me forever.

Peter was there and I brought through his brother again, this time describing the job he did, the clothes he was wearing, how he passed and he told me his name, Michael. A lovely message followed and Peter could take it all. Shortly after it was Peter's turn and he brought through his sister-in-law which we don't really do in circle as the messages are for others in the group but Stacey let this slide for some reason. Peter said that the message was indirectly for me but why? He described her as being surrounded by Egyptian artefacts as that was what she wanted to show me. At this point my ears were well pricked up and I began to tell Peter that I knew a lady like this who had moved to France, who's husband had been killed in a car accident following a heart attack and moved back to a bungalow in Ledbury and was very ill last time I saw her. Peter could take it all and I felt we were talking about the same person. I told him I had been trying to find a lady who had been my mentor through my spiritual journey and her name was Caroline Clare. He told me to sit down and then began by saying,

"My full name is Peter John Clare and Caroline was my sister-in-law", you could have knocked me down with a feather, he went on,

"Michael was Caroline's husband and my brother who died in the car accident, from a heart attack. She passed away a few years ago from cancer while living in the bungalow in Ledbury".

This tells me spirit are always around and if you ask them anything they can help. During that circle I felt her energies sit within me and now she is another guide, which does not surprise me.

I have sat in circle with Peter not knowing that he was the one person who could have linked me to Caroline Clare and I had not got a clue. Nobody else could have given the answer to that question that was eating me up and in all the circles in all of Britain he was sat next to me in mine. You can see why this had to be added onto the end of the book as you must agree it's amazing. Once again spirit has amazed me and I feel blessed to be able to work for them.

Good luck on all your journeys and may they be spiritual and amazing.

The End

Lightning Source UK Ltd.
Milton Keynes UK
UKOW03f0145070617
302829UK00001B/6/P